I0491588

MASTERPEACE MANDALAS

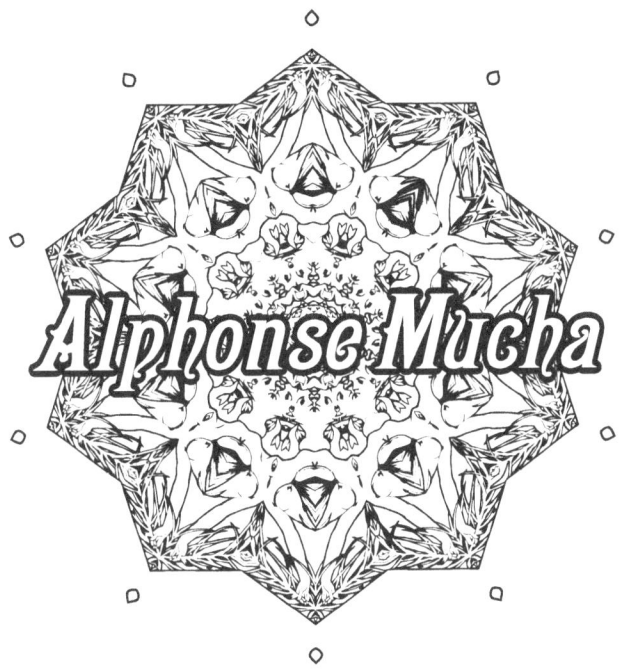

MUCHA
Coloring Book
VOLUME 1

This book does not recommend, promote or advise any diagnosis
or treatment for any condition and is not a substitute
for qualified professional consultation. But it could be fun.

Mucha Masterpeace Mandalas Coloring Book Volume 1

ISBN-10: 1944381058
ISBN-13: 978-1-944381-05-9

stop by and tell us what you think
www.masterpeacebooks.com

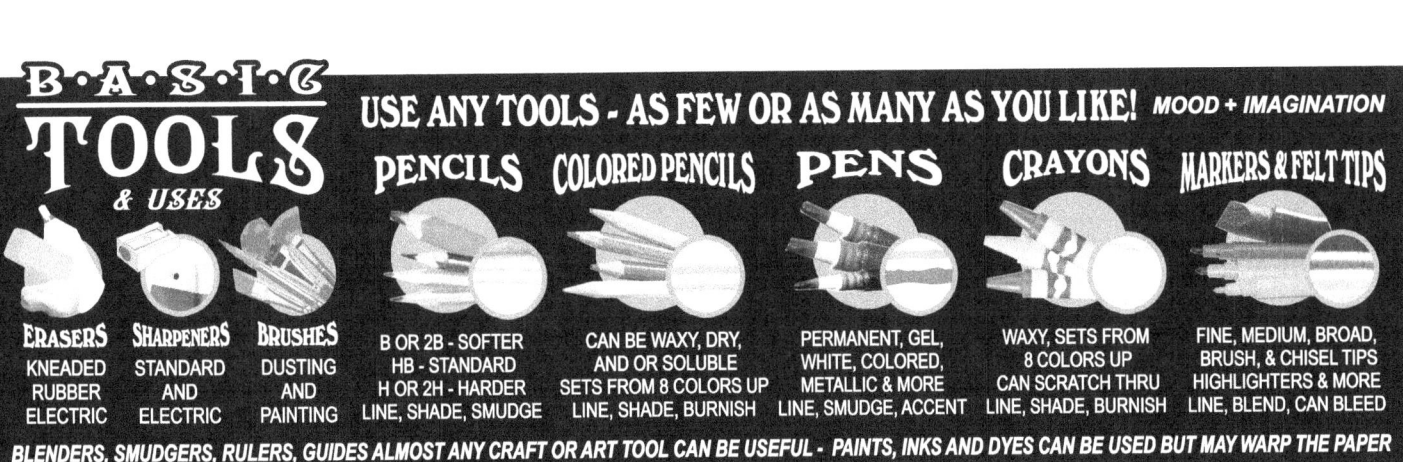

B·A·S·I·C TOOLS & USES

USE ANY TOOLS - AS FEW OR AS MANY AS YOU LIKE! *MOOD + IMAGINATION*

PENCILS · **COLORED PENCILS** · **PENS** · **CRAYONS** · **MARKERS & FELT TIPS**

ERASERS	SHARPENERS	BRUSHES	PENCILS	COLORED PENCILS	PENS	CRAYONS	MARKERS & FELT TIPS
KNEADED RUBBER ELECTRIC	STANDARD AND ELECTRIC	DUSTING AND PAINTING	B OR 2B - SOFTER HB - STANDARD H OR 2H - HARDER LINE, SHADE, SMUDGE	CAN BE WAXY, DRY, AND OR SOLUBLE SETS FROM 8 COLORS UP LINE, SHADE, BURNISH	PERMANENT, GEL, WHITE, COLORED, METALLIC & MORE LINE, SMUDGE, ACCENT	WAXY, SETS FROM 8 COLORS UP CAN SCRATCH THRU LINE, SHADE, BURNISH	FINE, MEDIUM, BROAD, BRUSH, & CHISEL TIPS HIGHLIGHTERS & MORE LINE, BLEND, CAN BLEED

BLENDERS, SMUDGERS, RULERS, GUIDES ALMOST ANY CRAFT OR ART TOOL CAN BE USEFUL - PAINTS, INKS AND DYES CAN BE USED BUT MAY WARP THE PAPER

B·A·S·I·C TECHNIQUES

INSIDE & OUTSIDE THE LINES

USE EVERY TYPE OF MEDIA YOU HAVE OR ONLY ONE *WHATEVER YOU FEEL*

STIPPLE USE THE TIP OR POINT TO MAKE DOTS

SCUMBLE TEXTURE W/ RANDOM OVERLAPPED CIRCLES

BURNISH LAYER WITH HEAVY PRESSURE

LINES
SHARP = FINE   BLUNT = THICK

HATCHING ONE DIRECTION

CROSS HATCHING TWO + DIRECTIONS

DRAW PATTERNS ANY SHAPE WILL DO

BLEND
COLOR TO COLOR   VALUE TO VALUE

LAYERING USE LIGHT PRESSURE

ADD BLACK OR WHITE SHADE & TINT ANY COLOR

COLORLESS BLENDER SMOOTH OUT TONES

FORM

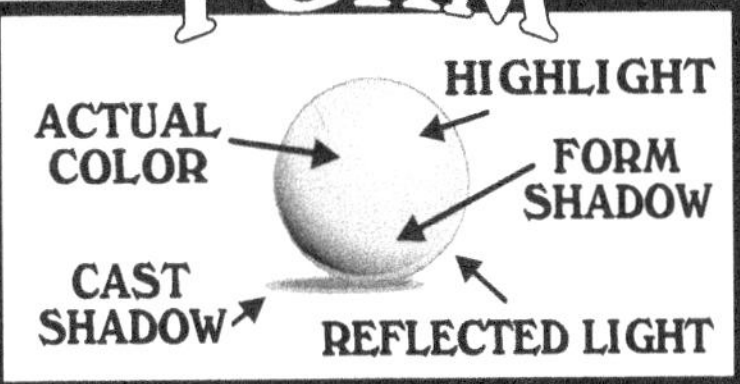

ACTUAL COLOR
HIGHLIGHT
FORM SHADOW
CAST SHADOW
REFLECTED LIGHT

FILL SOLID   **GRADUATE** TONE   **GRADUATE** COLOR   **TIP** TEST COLORING IDEAS

REMEMBER THESE ARE SUGGESTIONS TO INSPIRE YOUR CREATIVITY, THERE IS NO RIGHT OR WRONG

TESTING AREA BELOW - COMBINE MEDIA - PRACTICE - DOODLE IN THE MARGINS - CHECK POINTS - TAKE NOTES - TANGLE - SCRIBBLE

Tip - Carefully Remove The Last Page Of This Book And Place It Under The Page Your Working On To Protect The Next Page

REMEMBER THERE IS NO RIGHT OR WRONG WAY TO COLOR - COLOR HOW YOU FEEL - WHEN YOU FEEL - AND AS LONG AS YOU FEEL

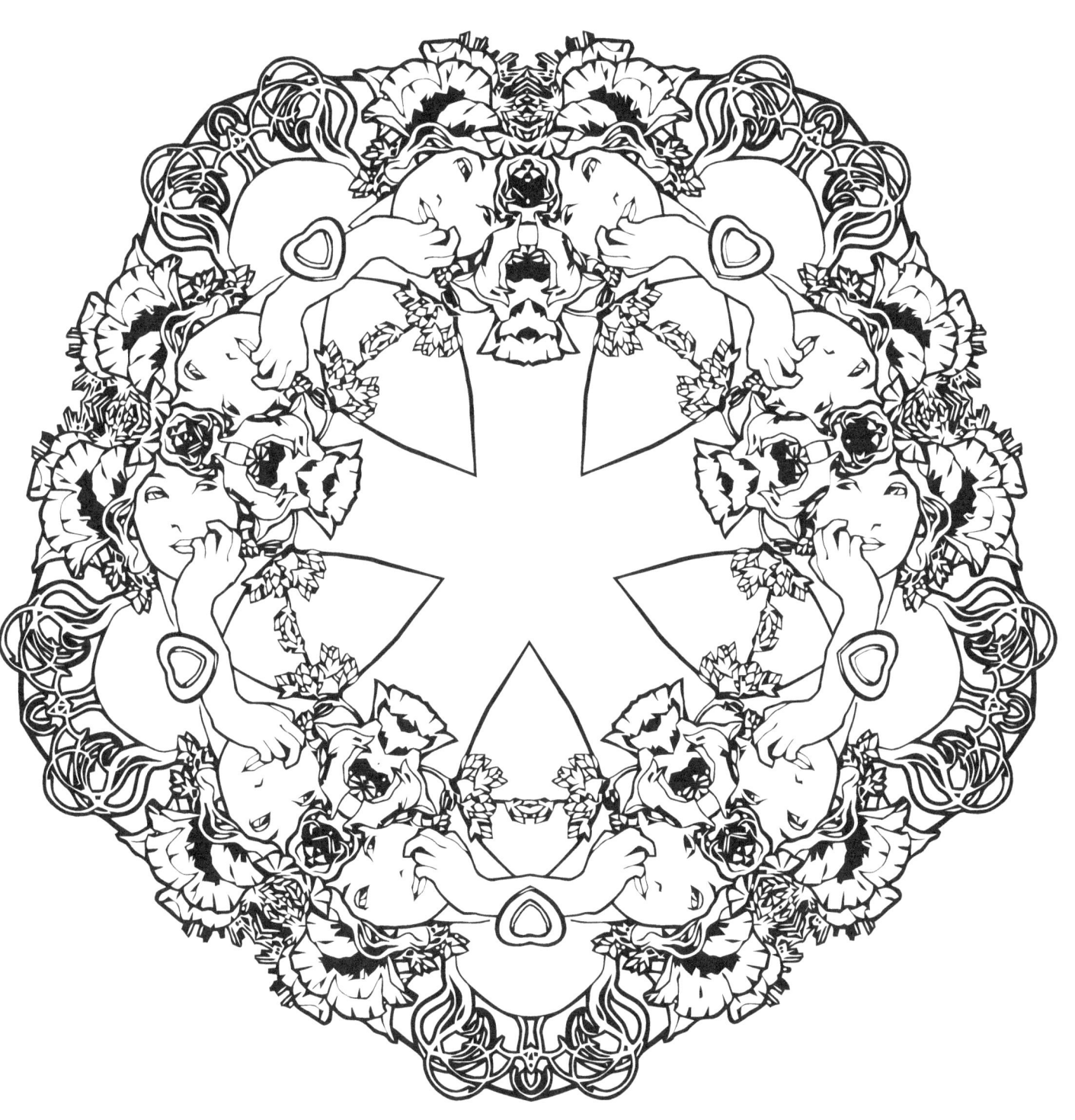

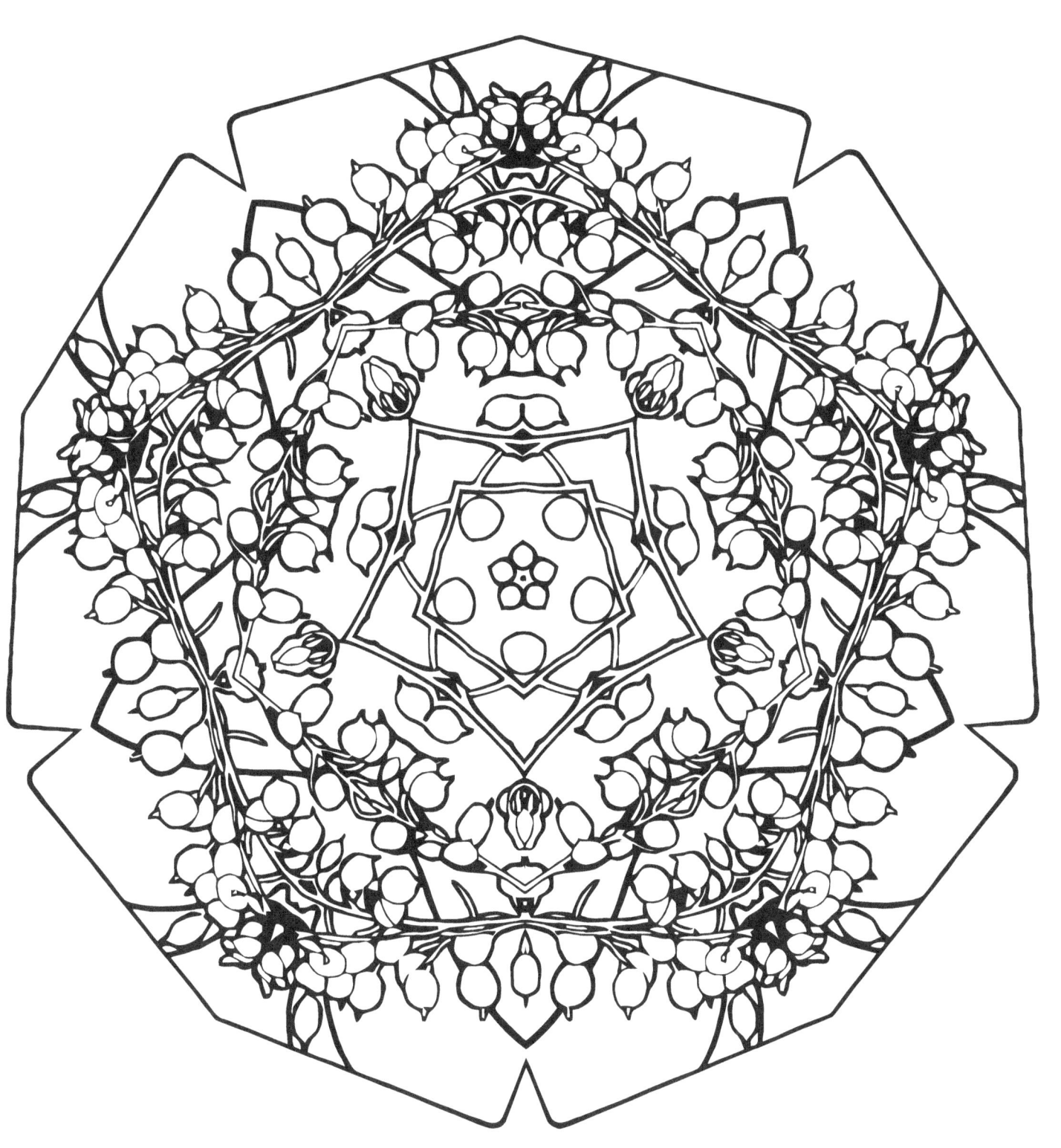

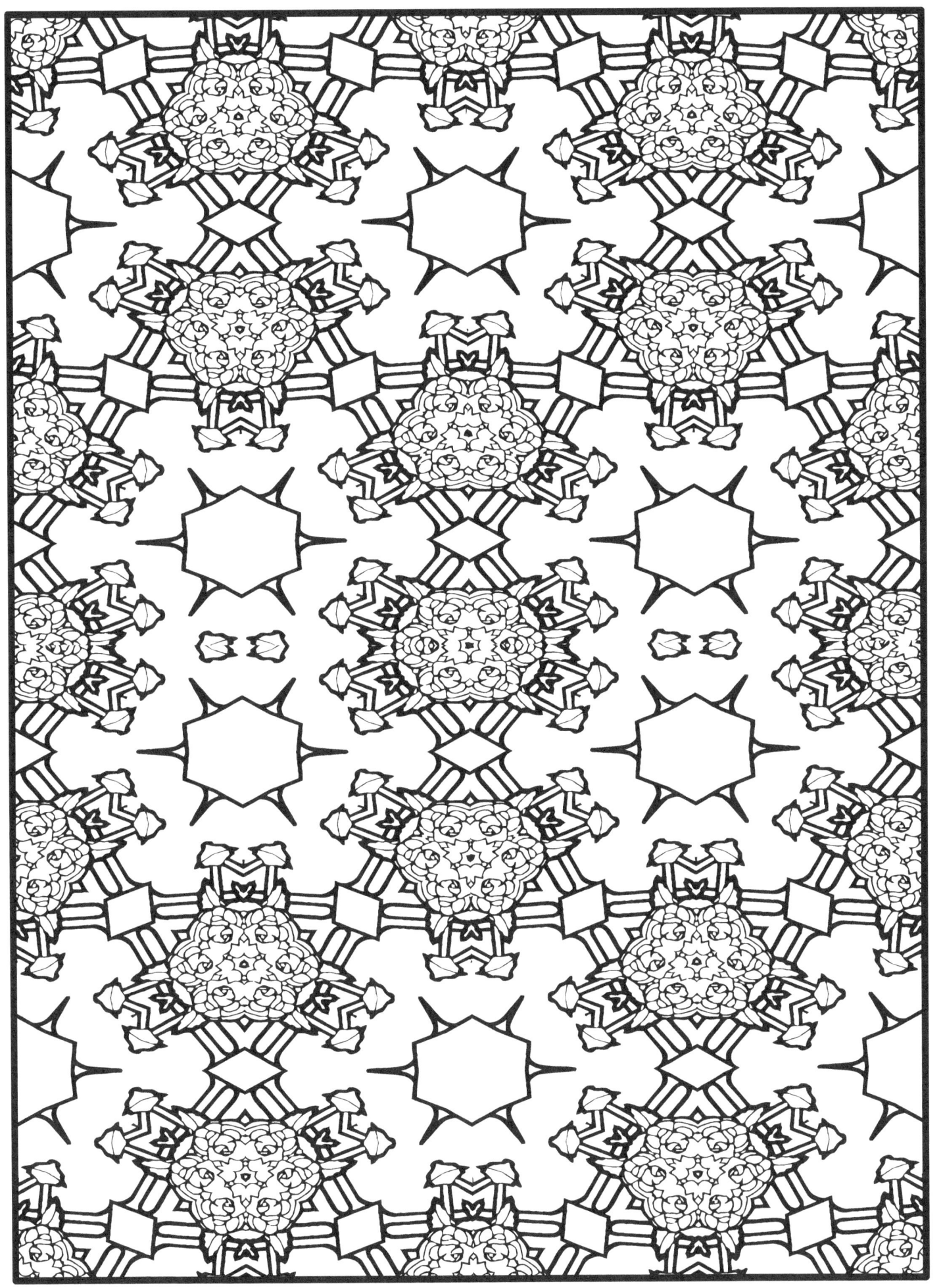

.

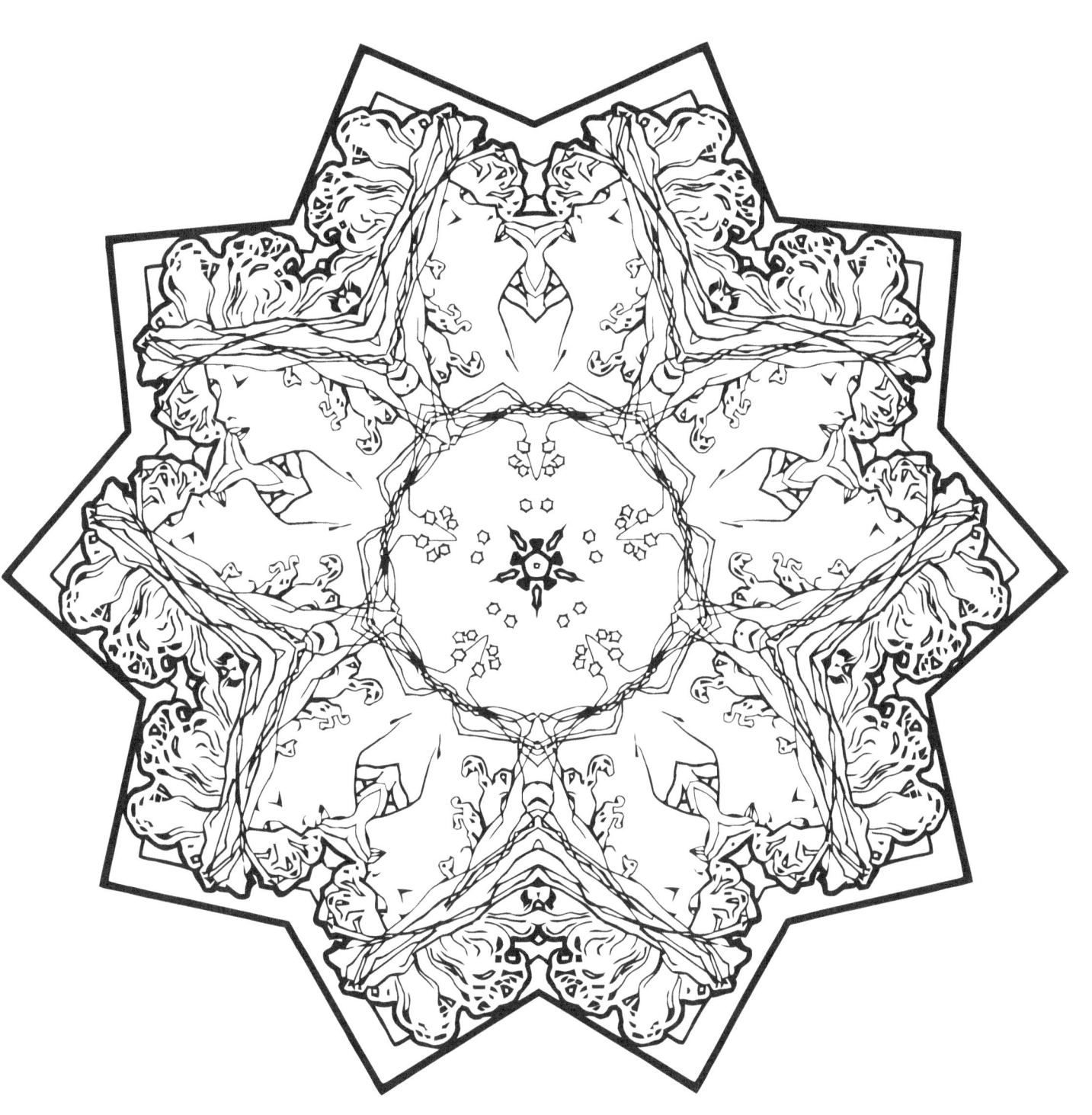

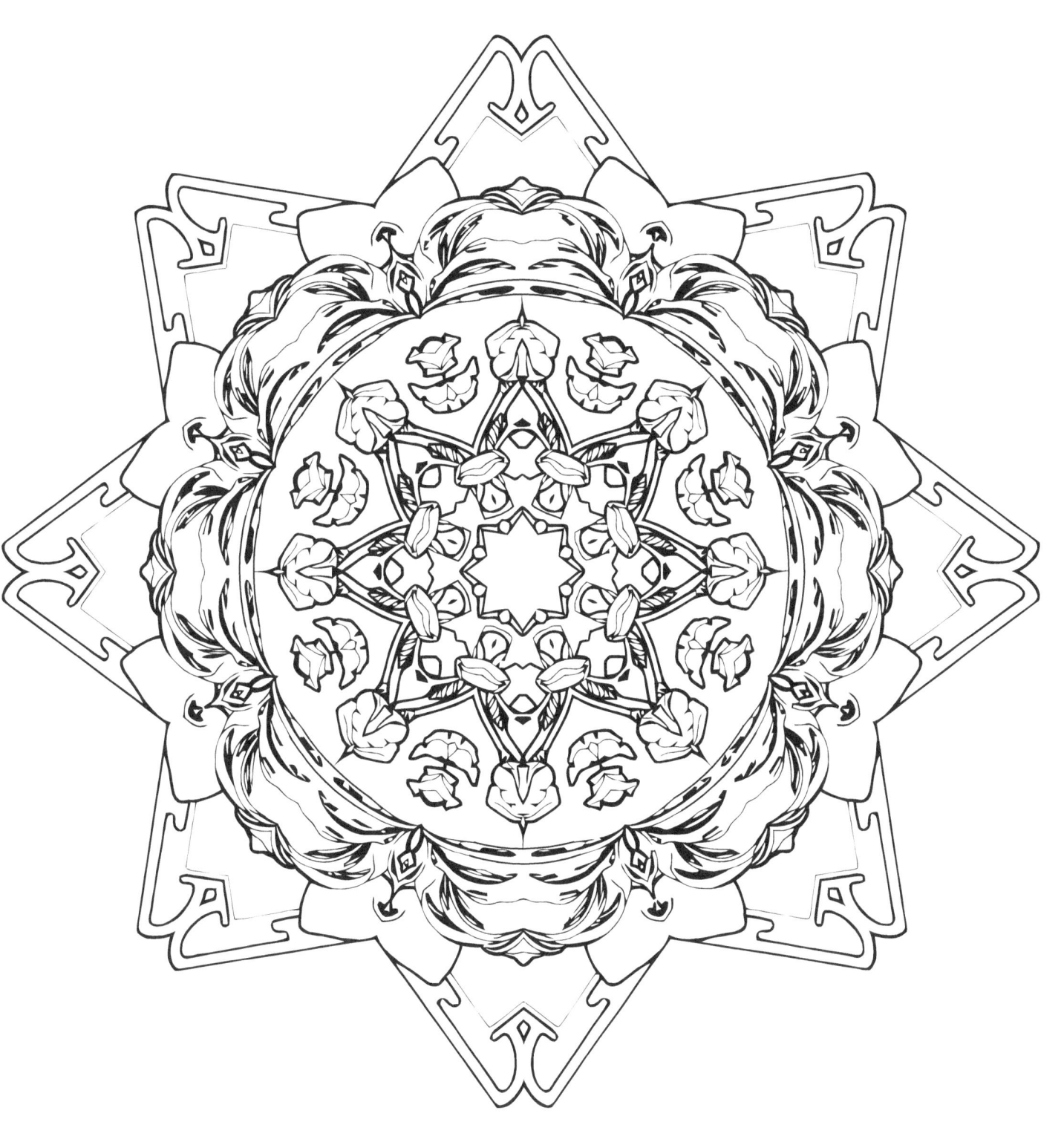

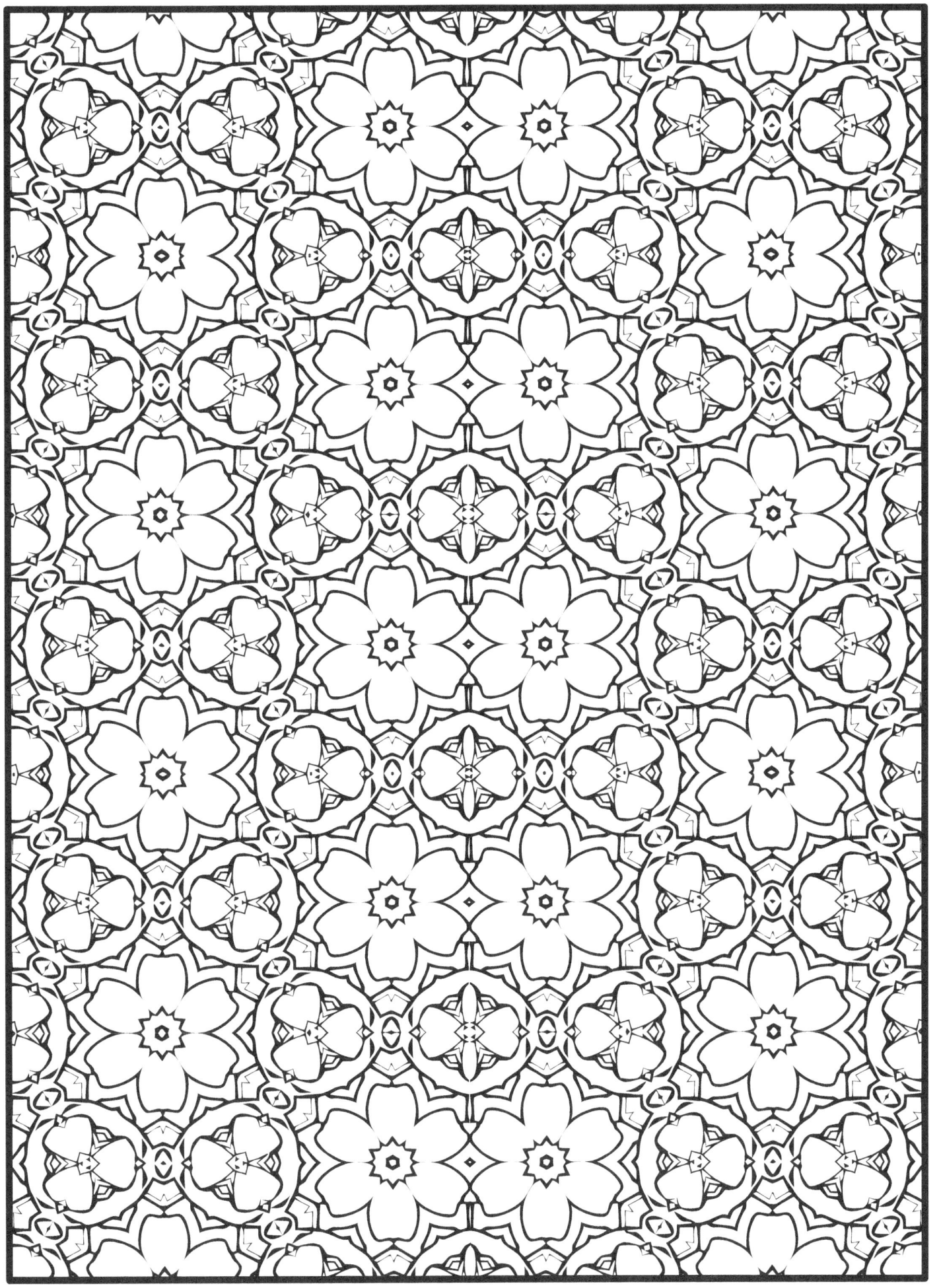

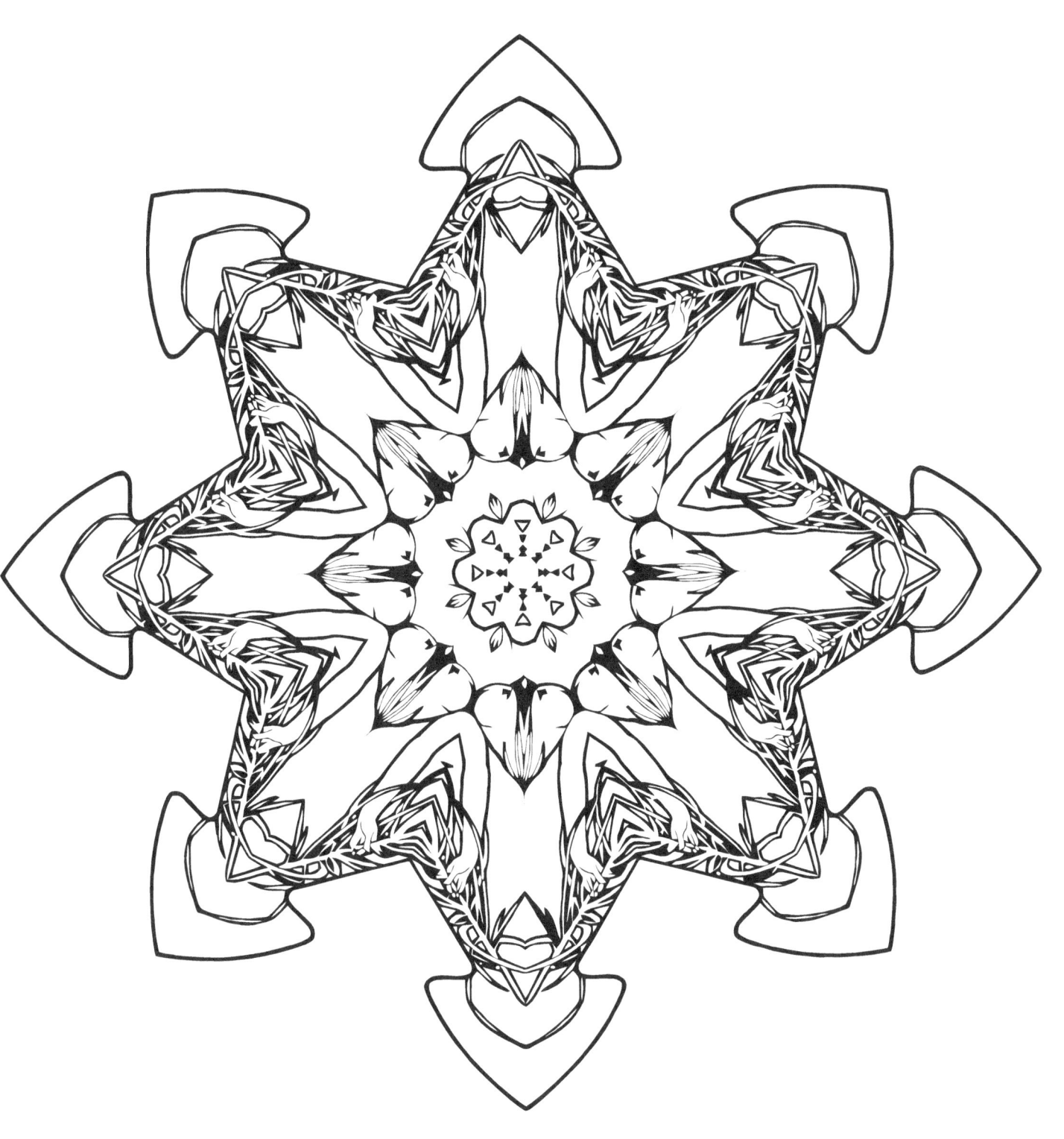

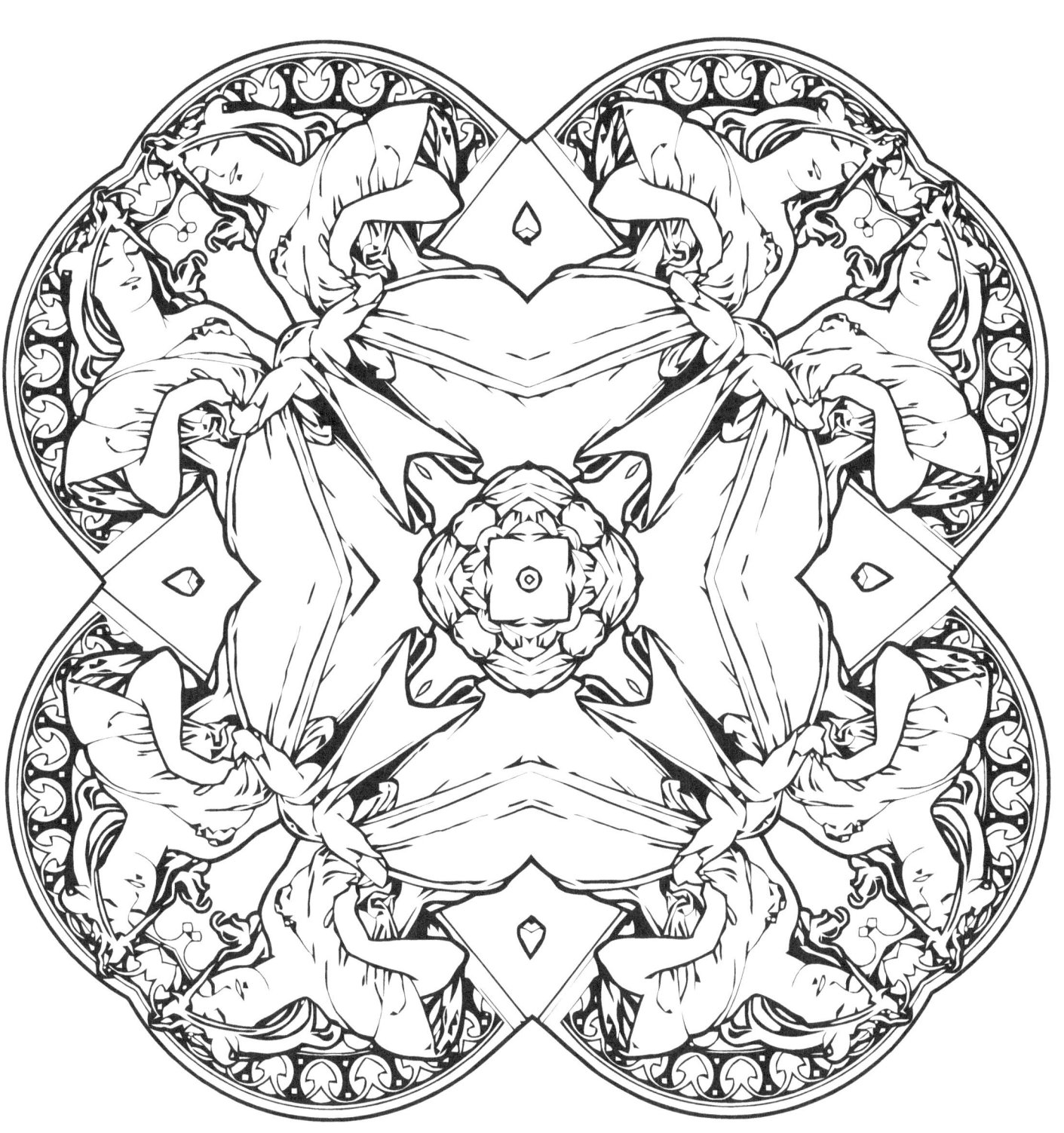

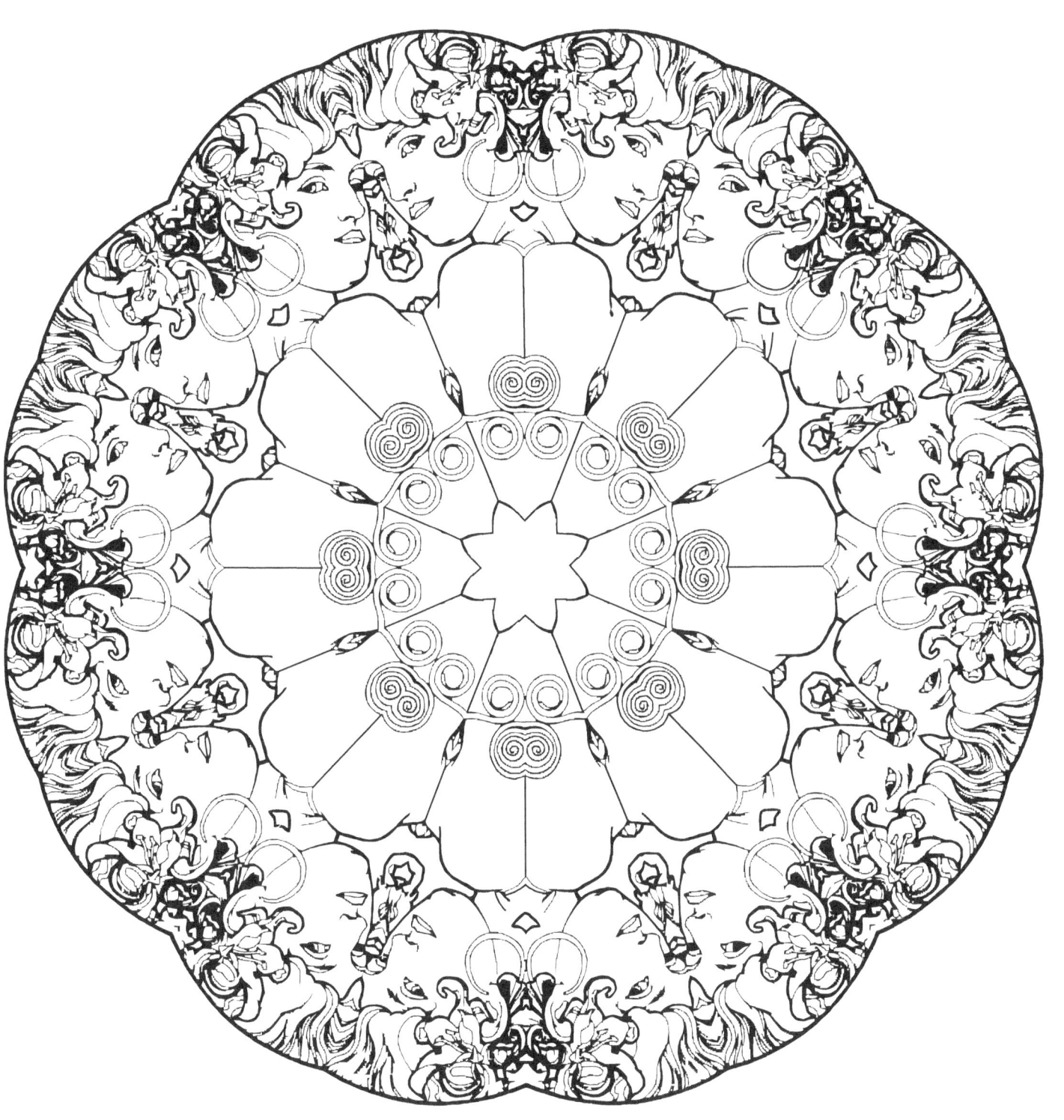

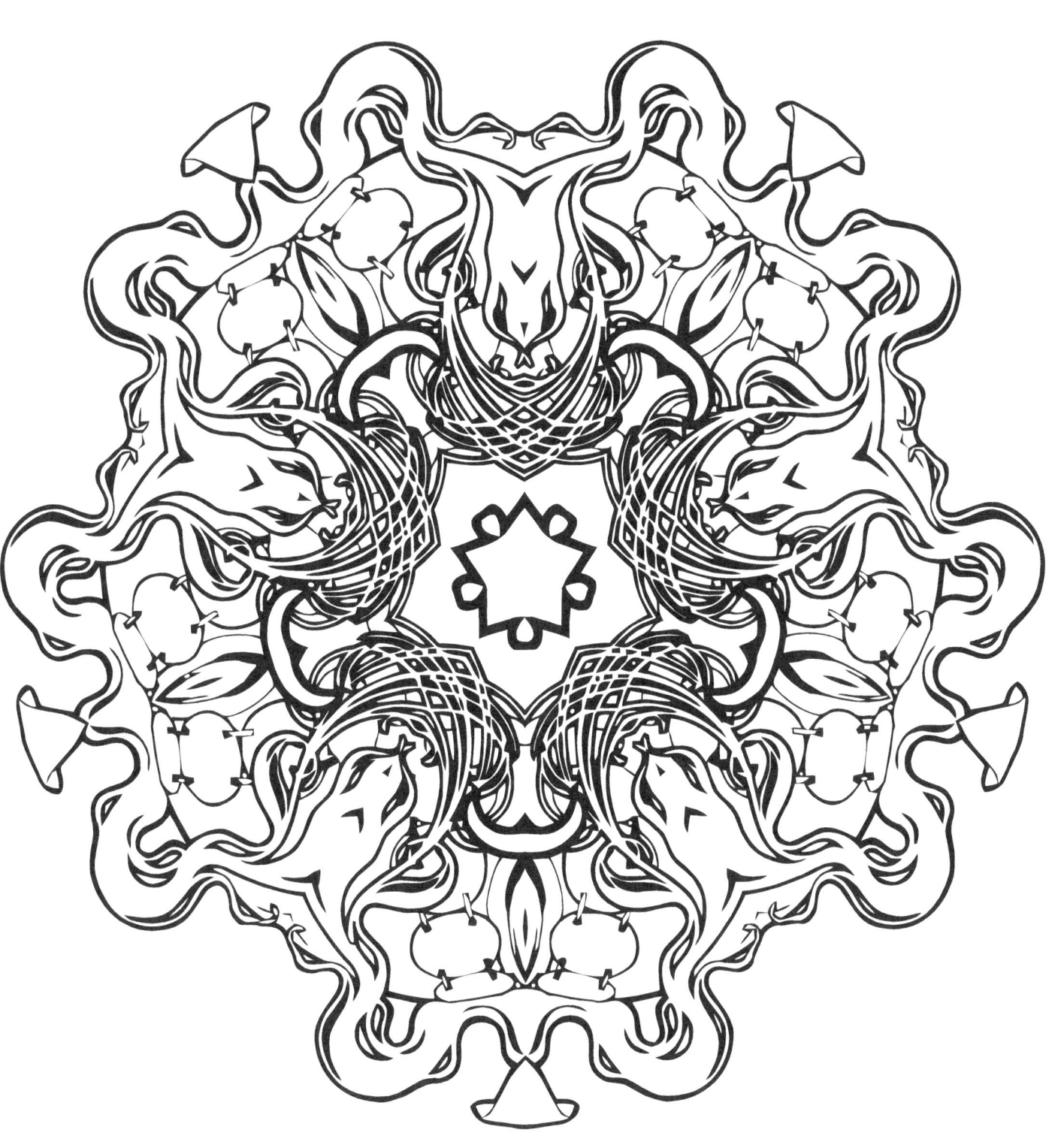

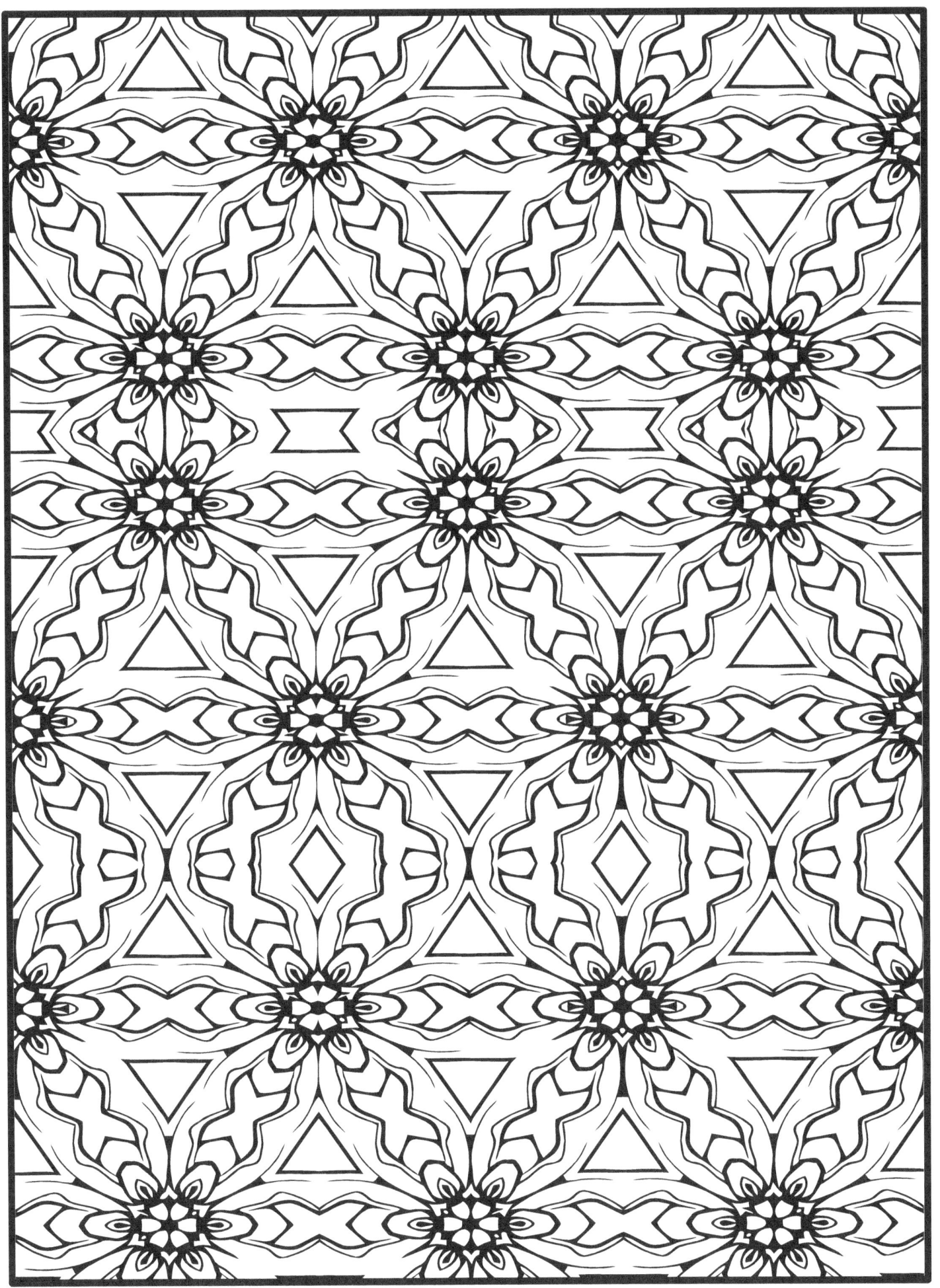

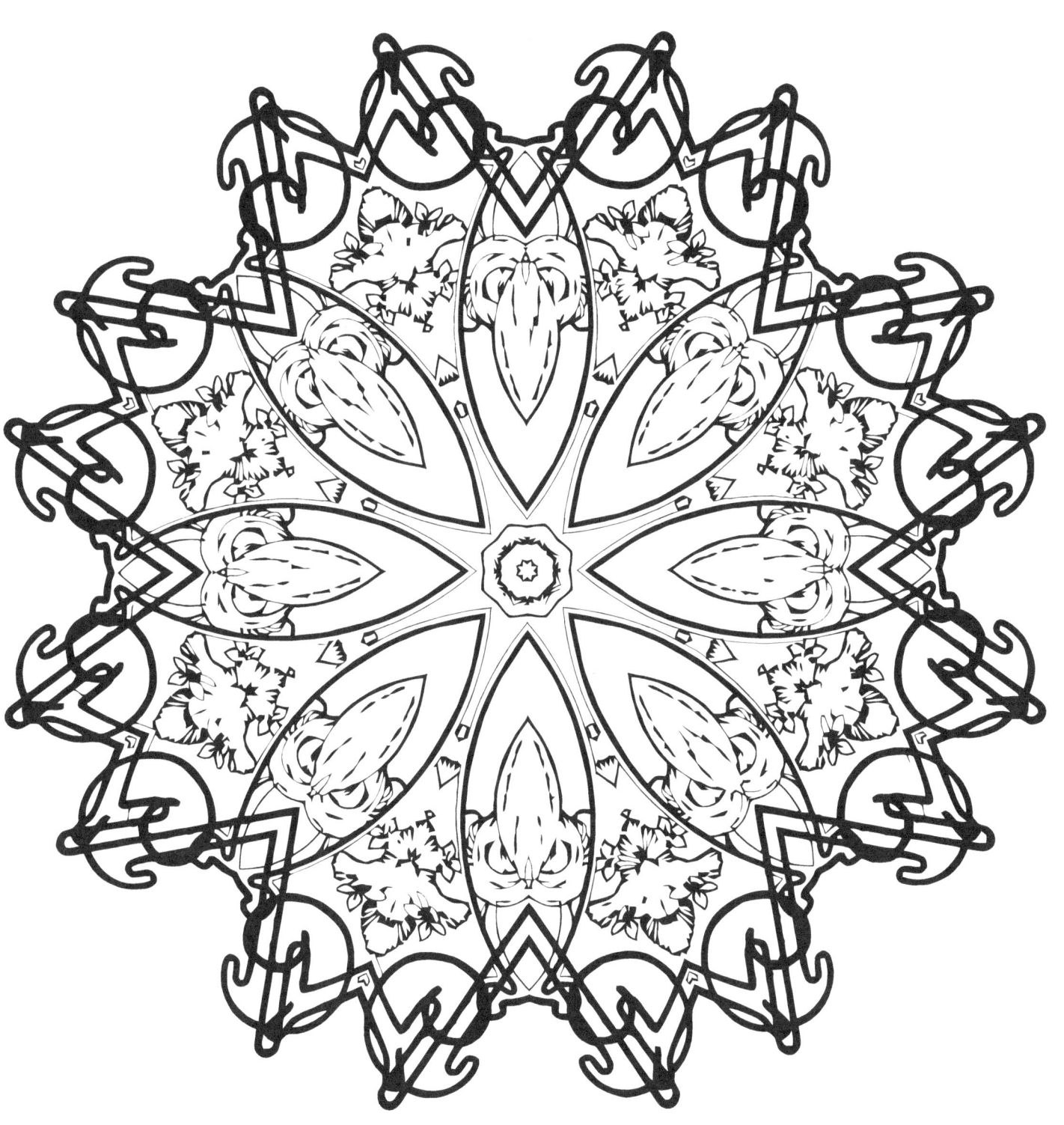

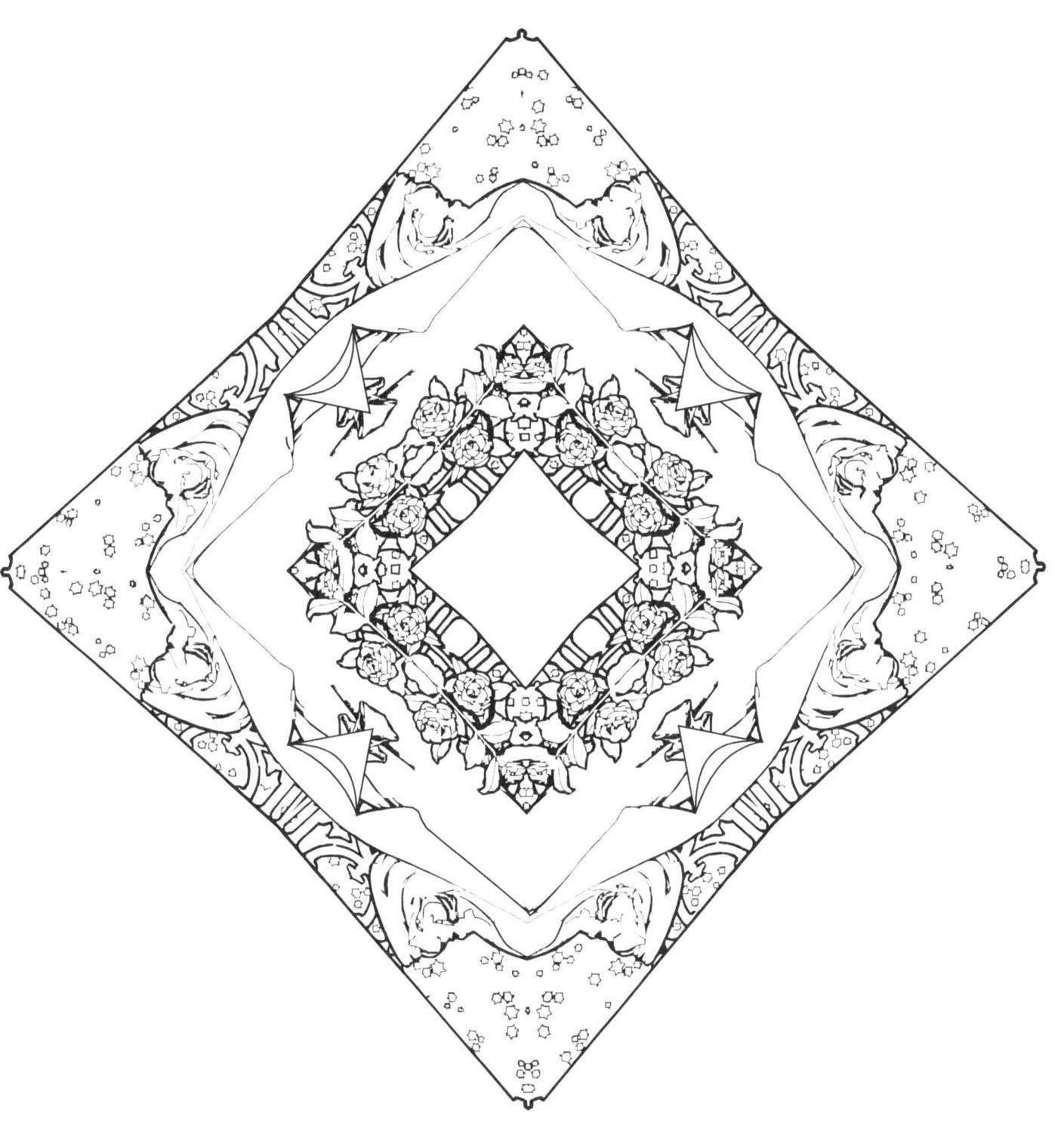

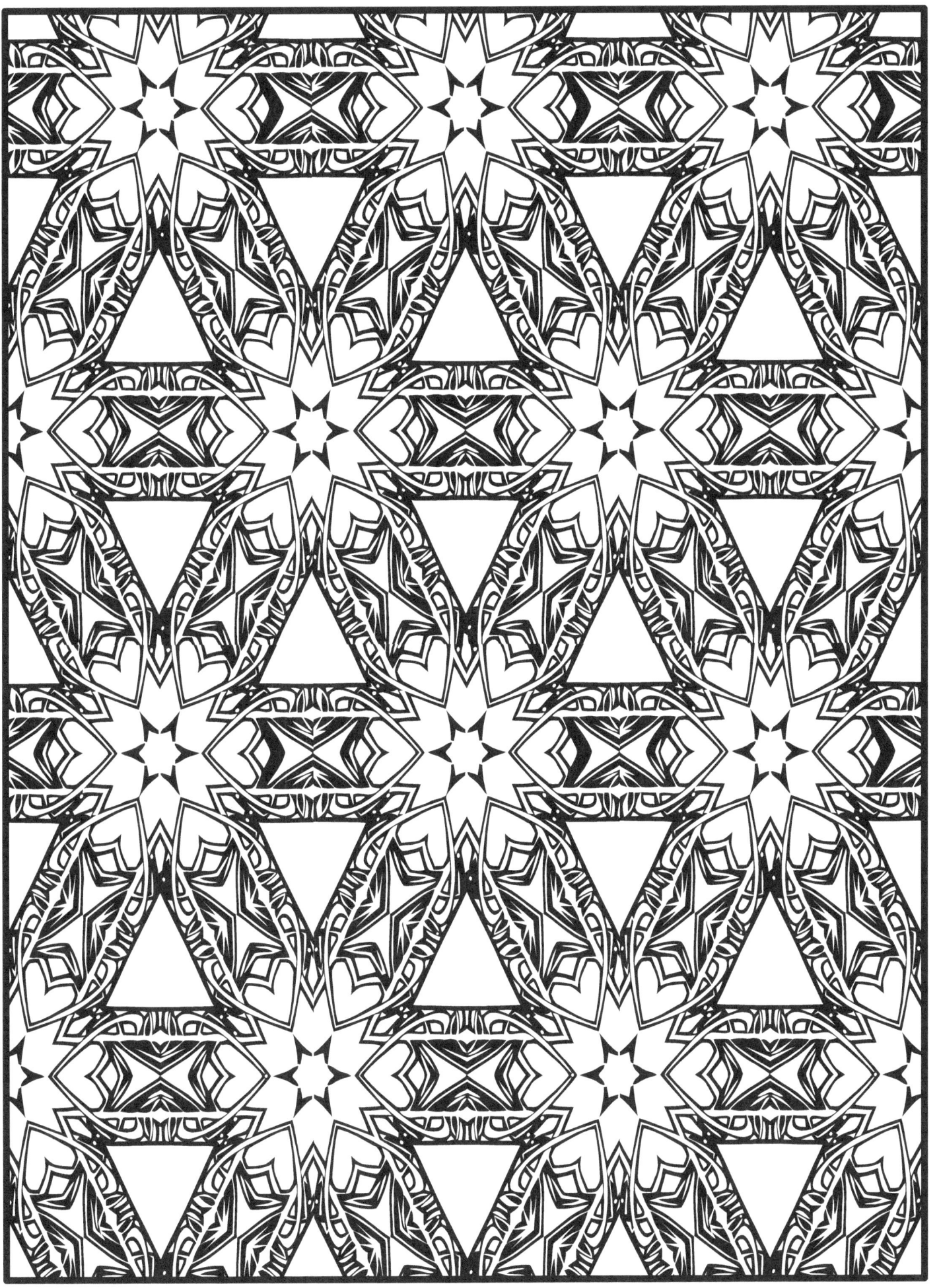

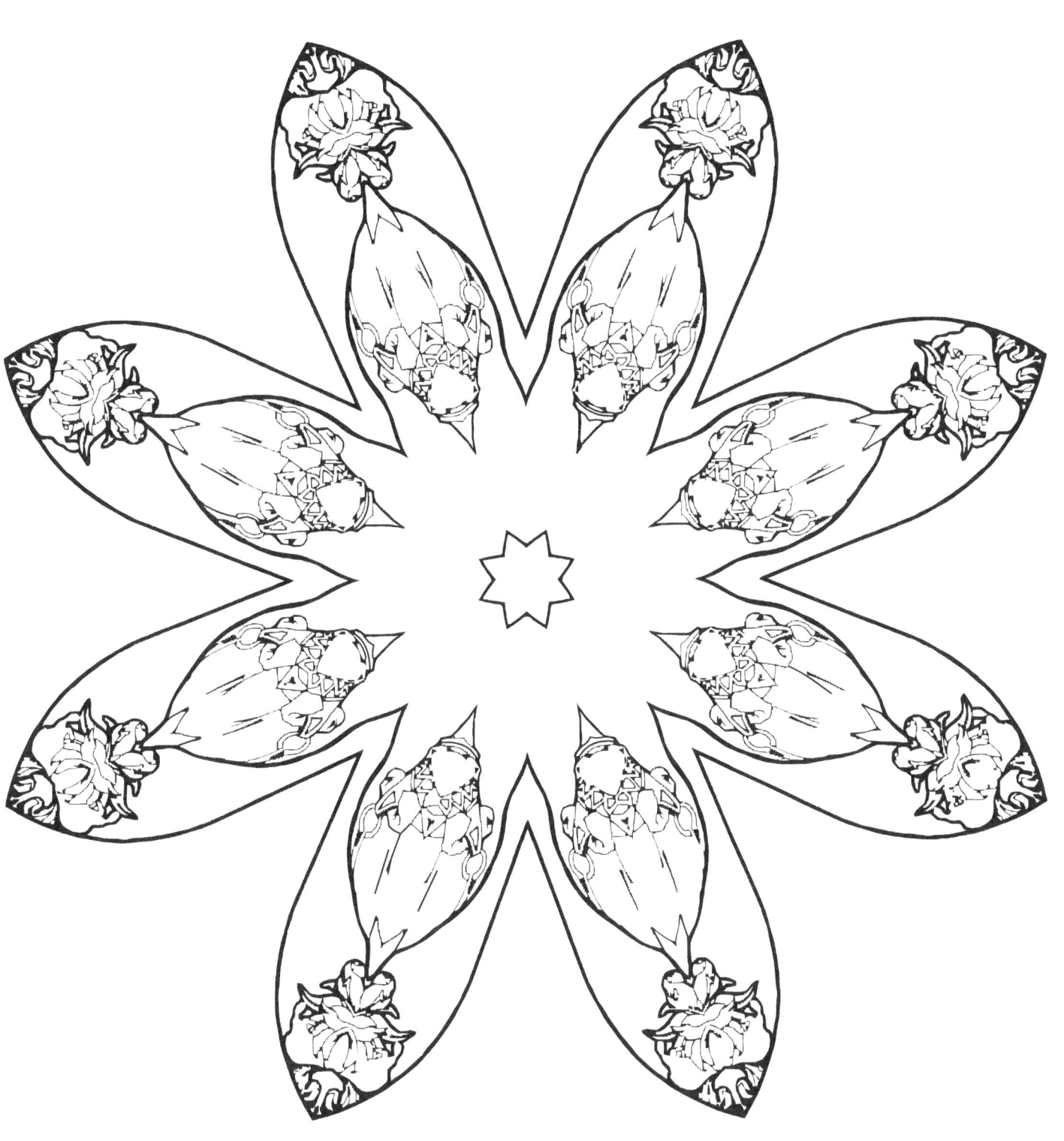

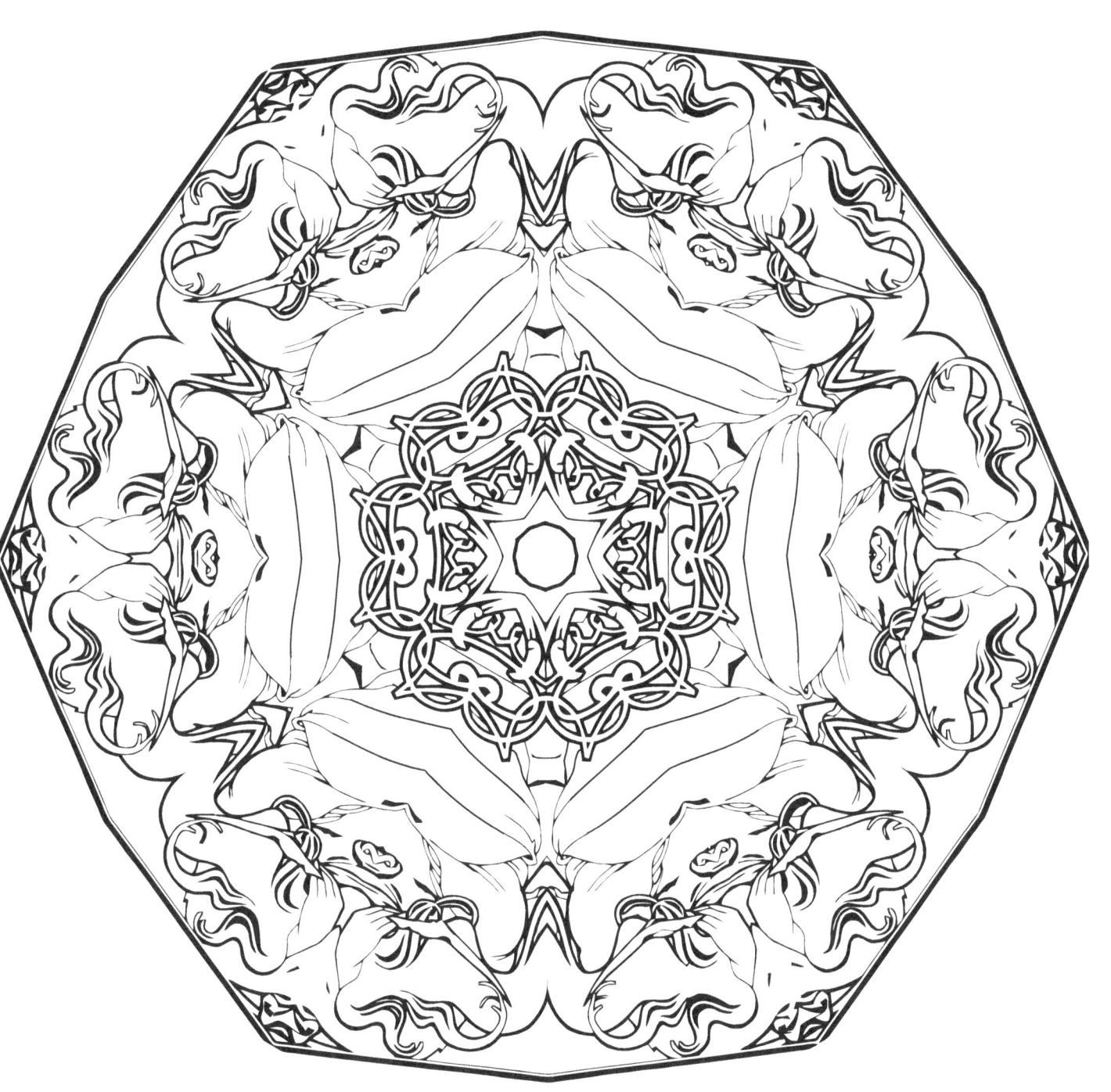

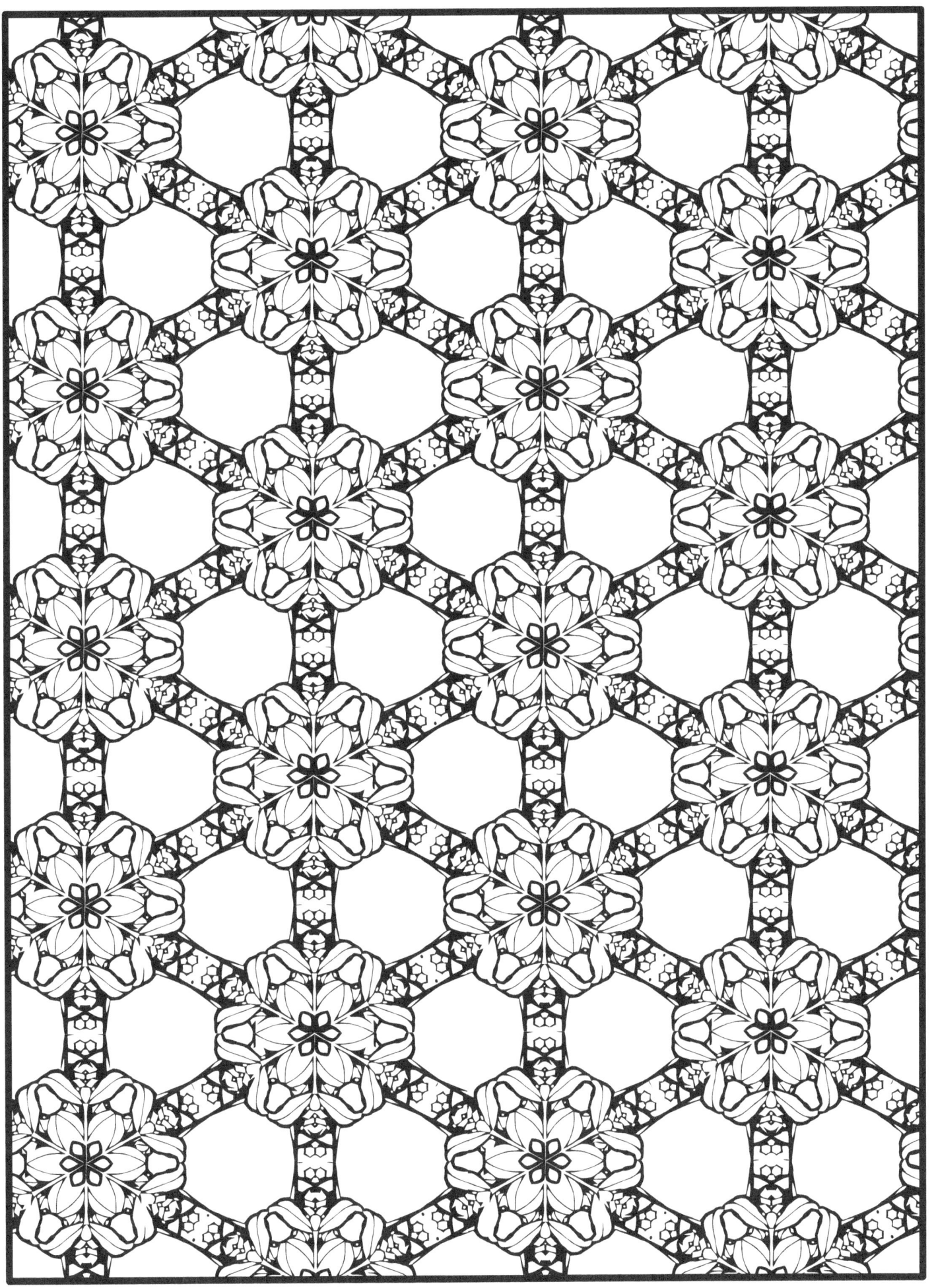

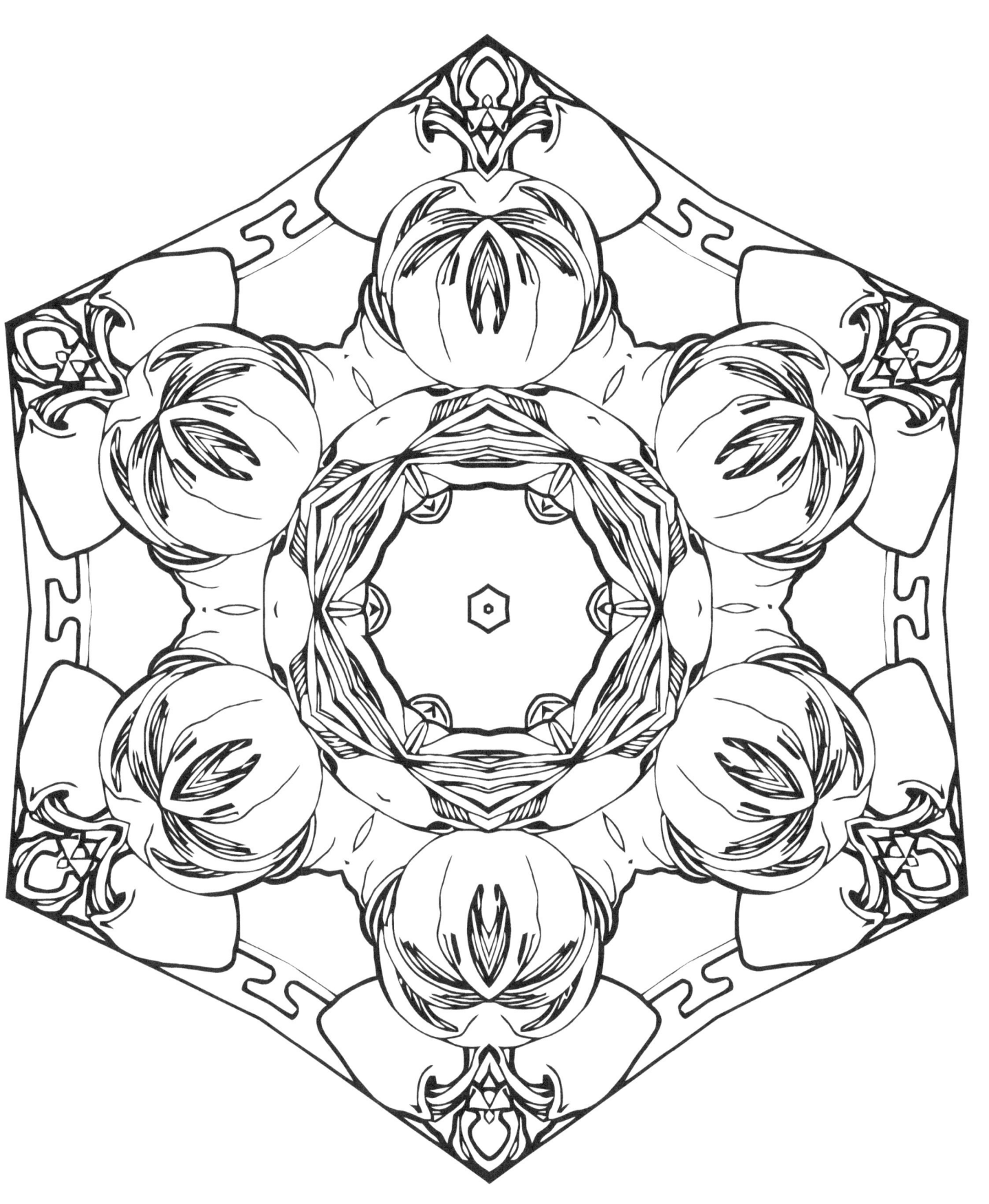

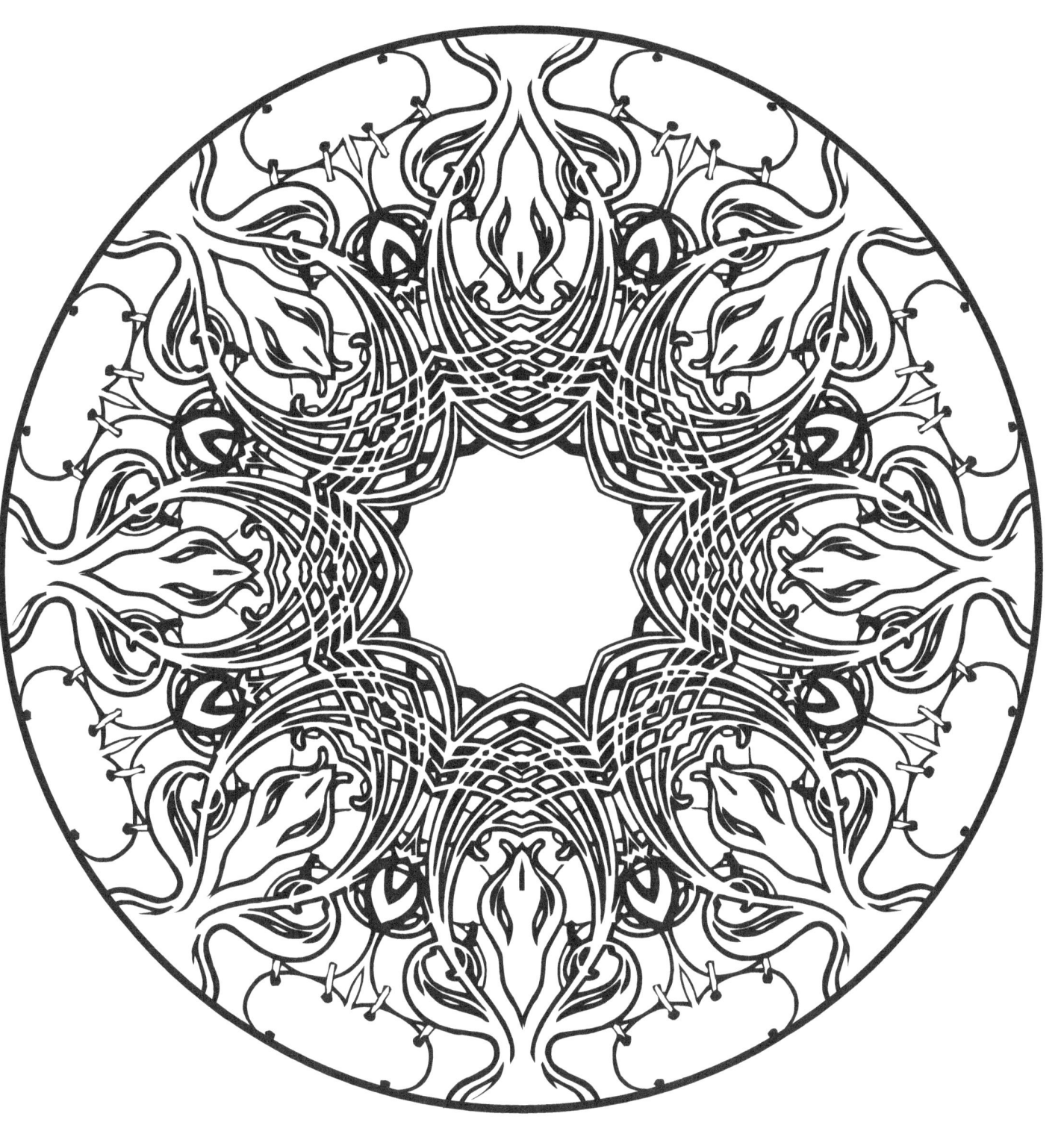

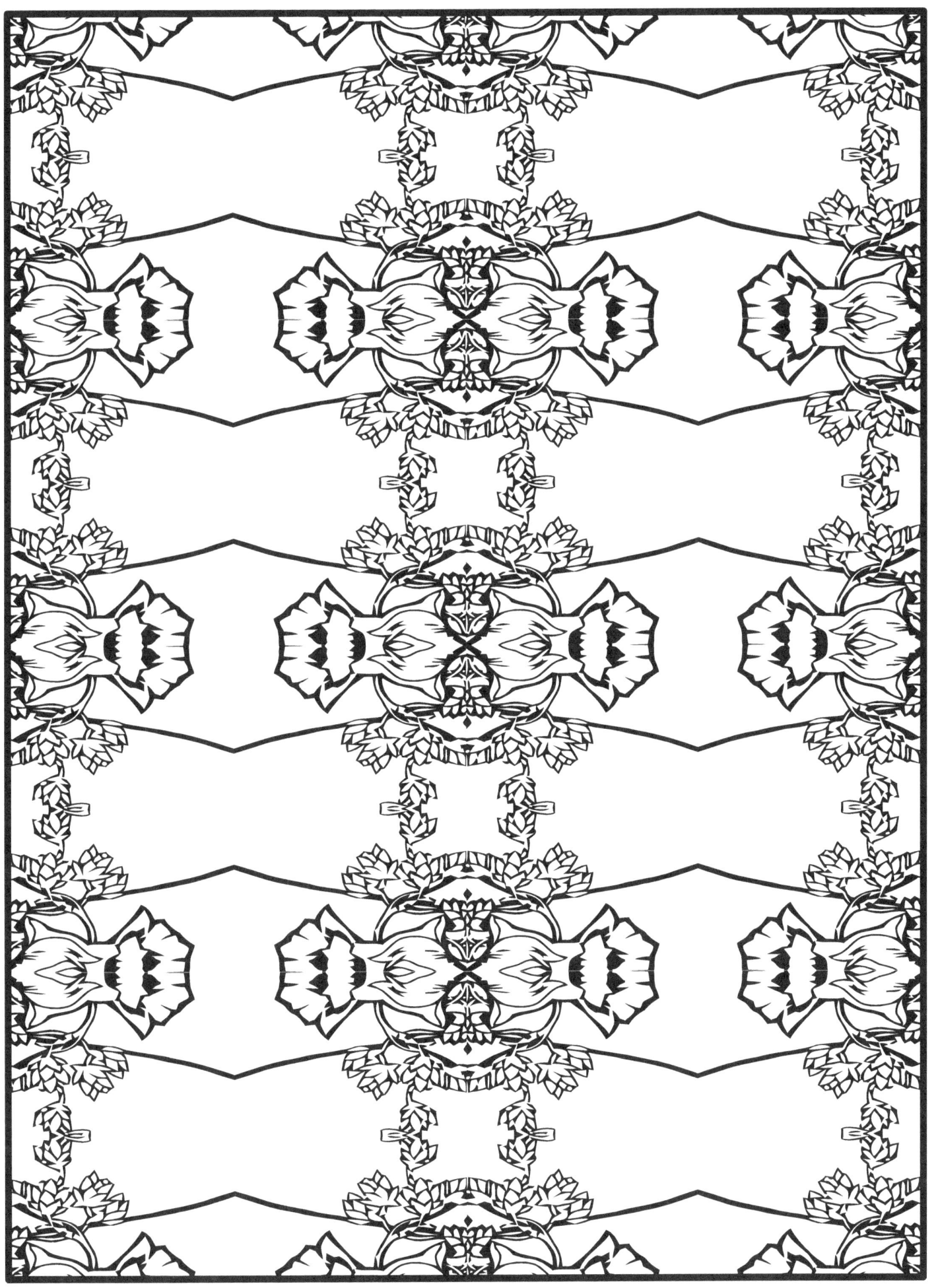

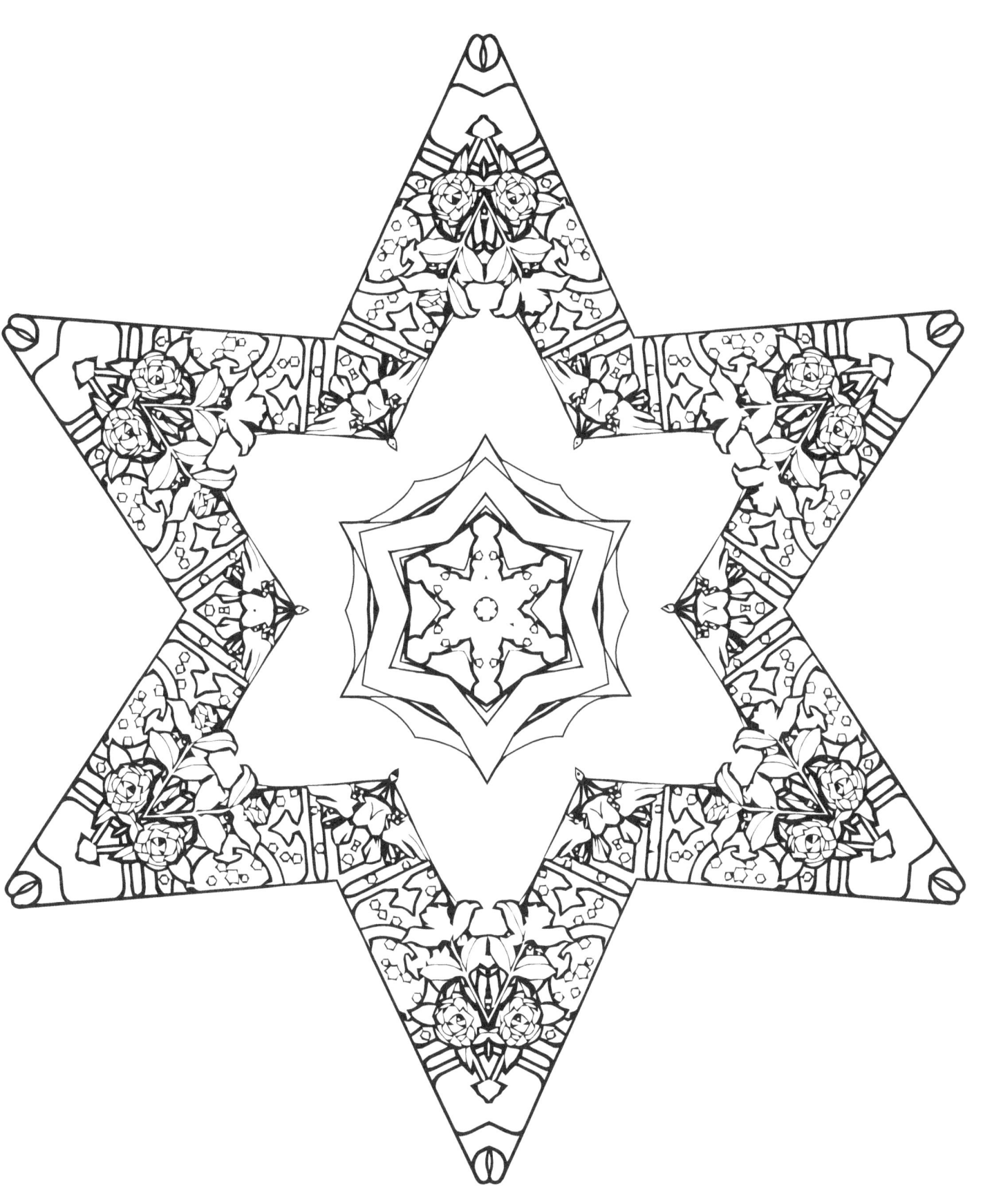

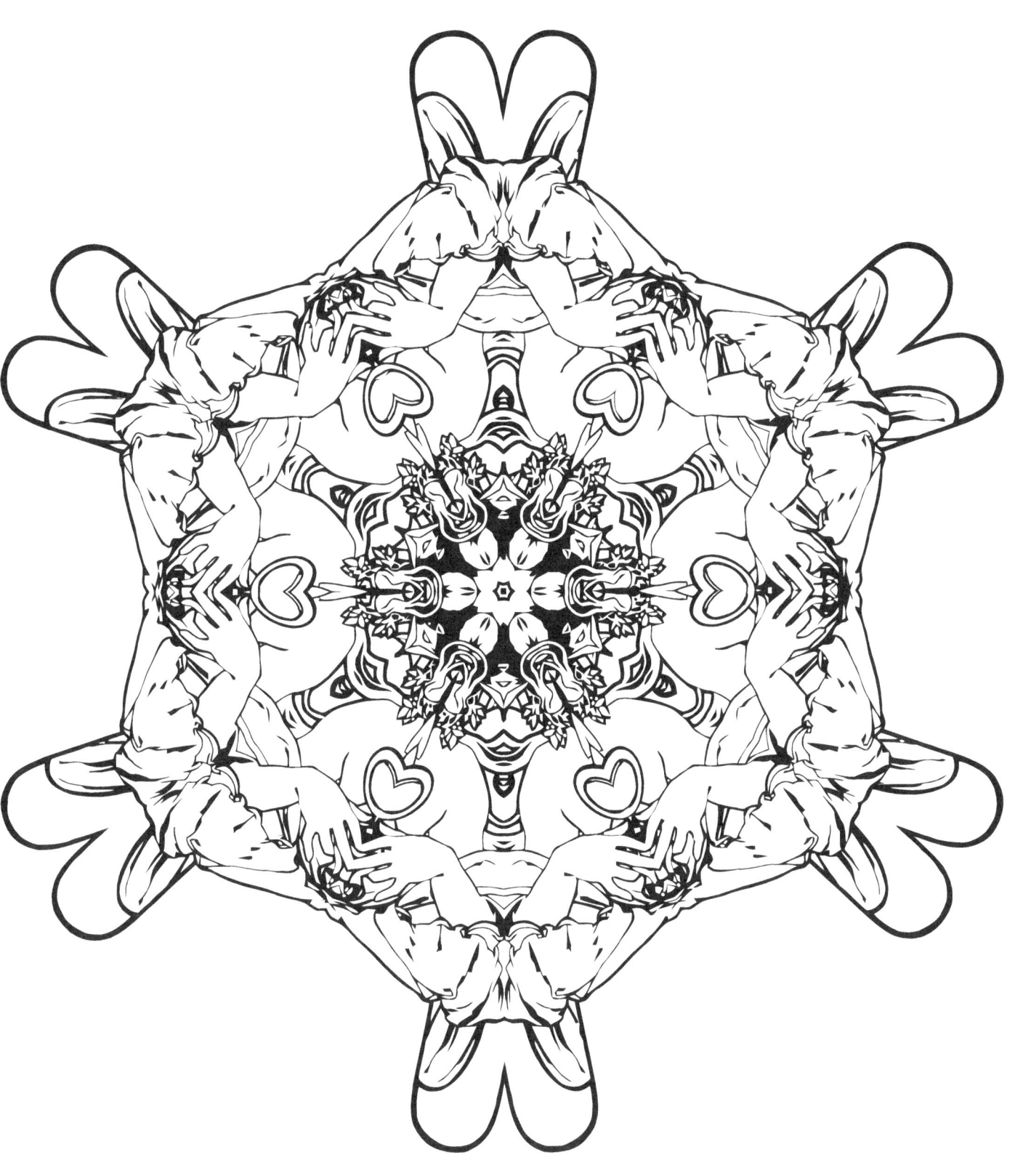

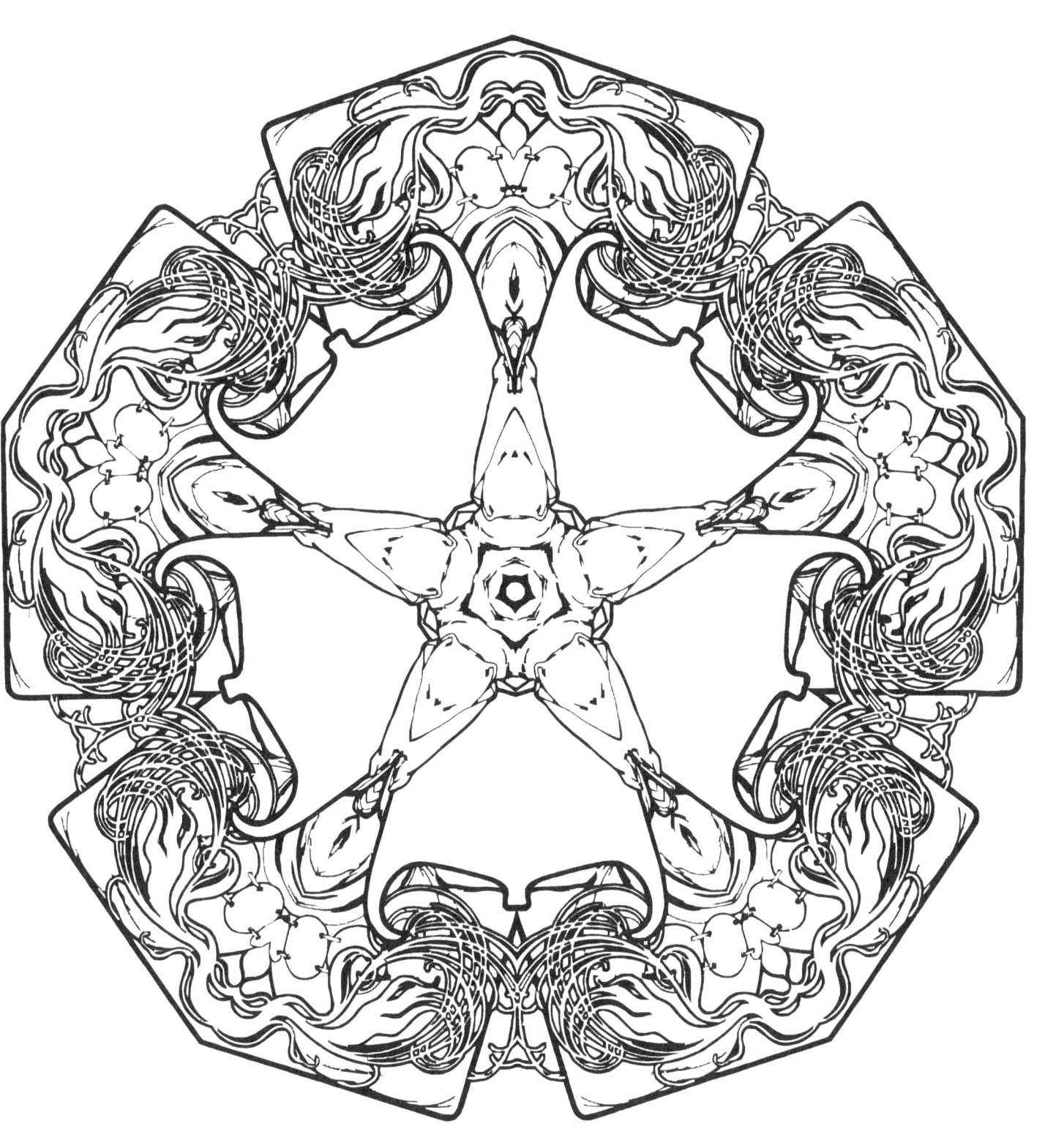

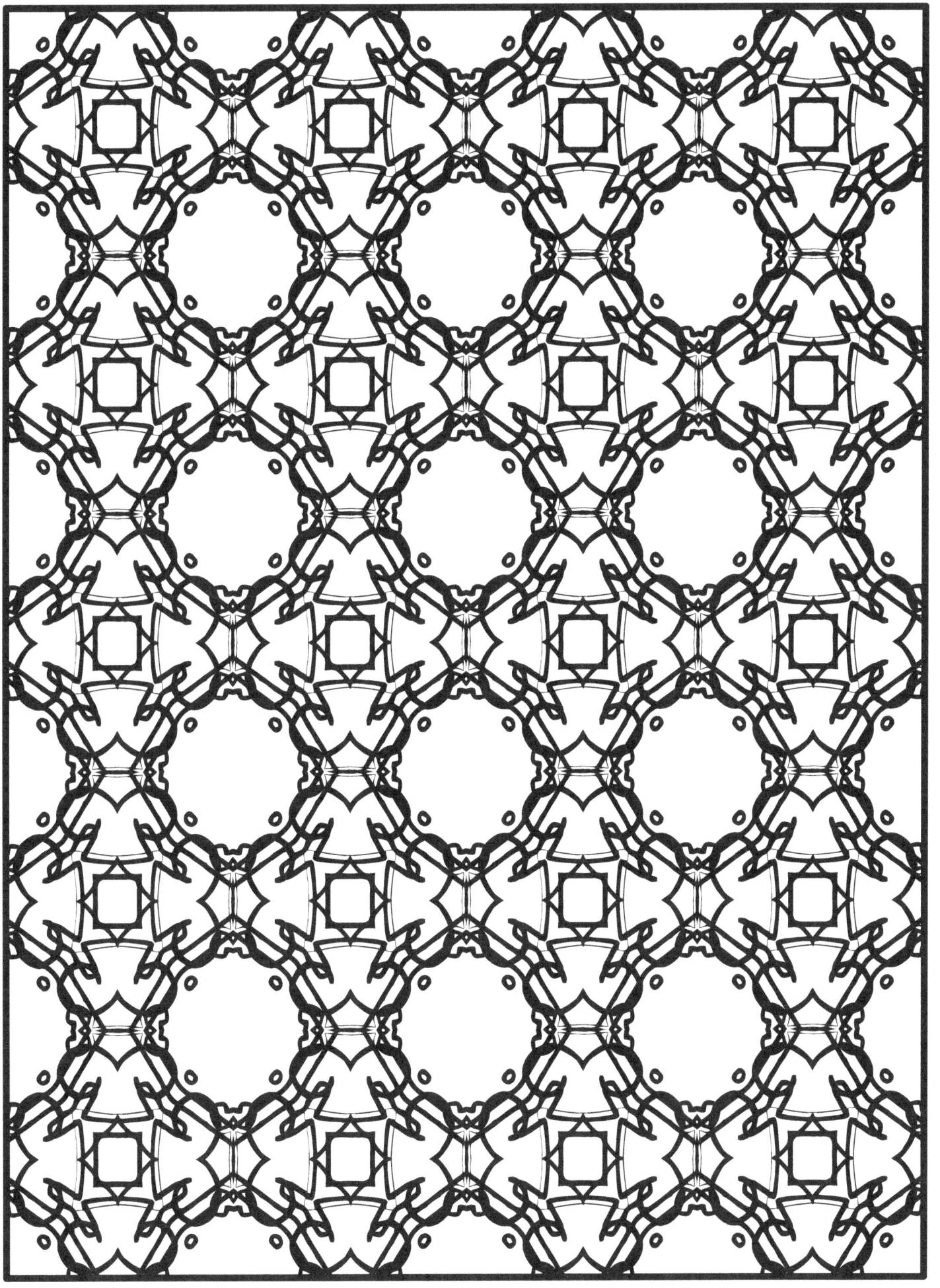

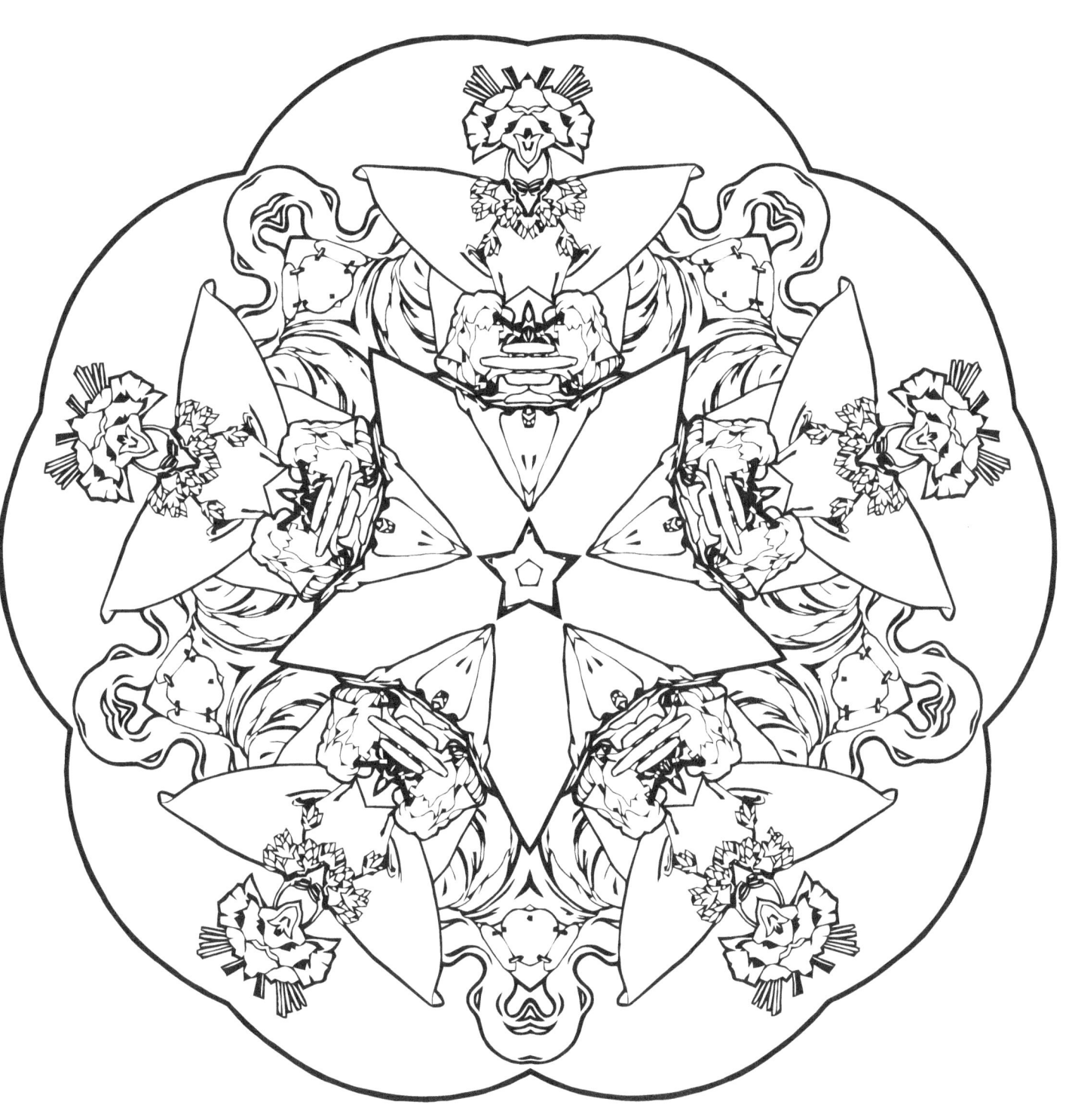

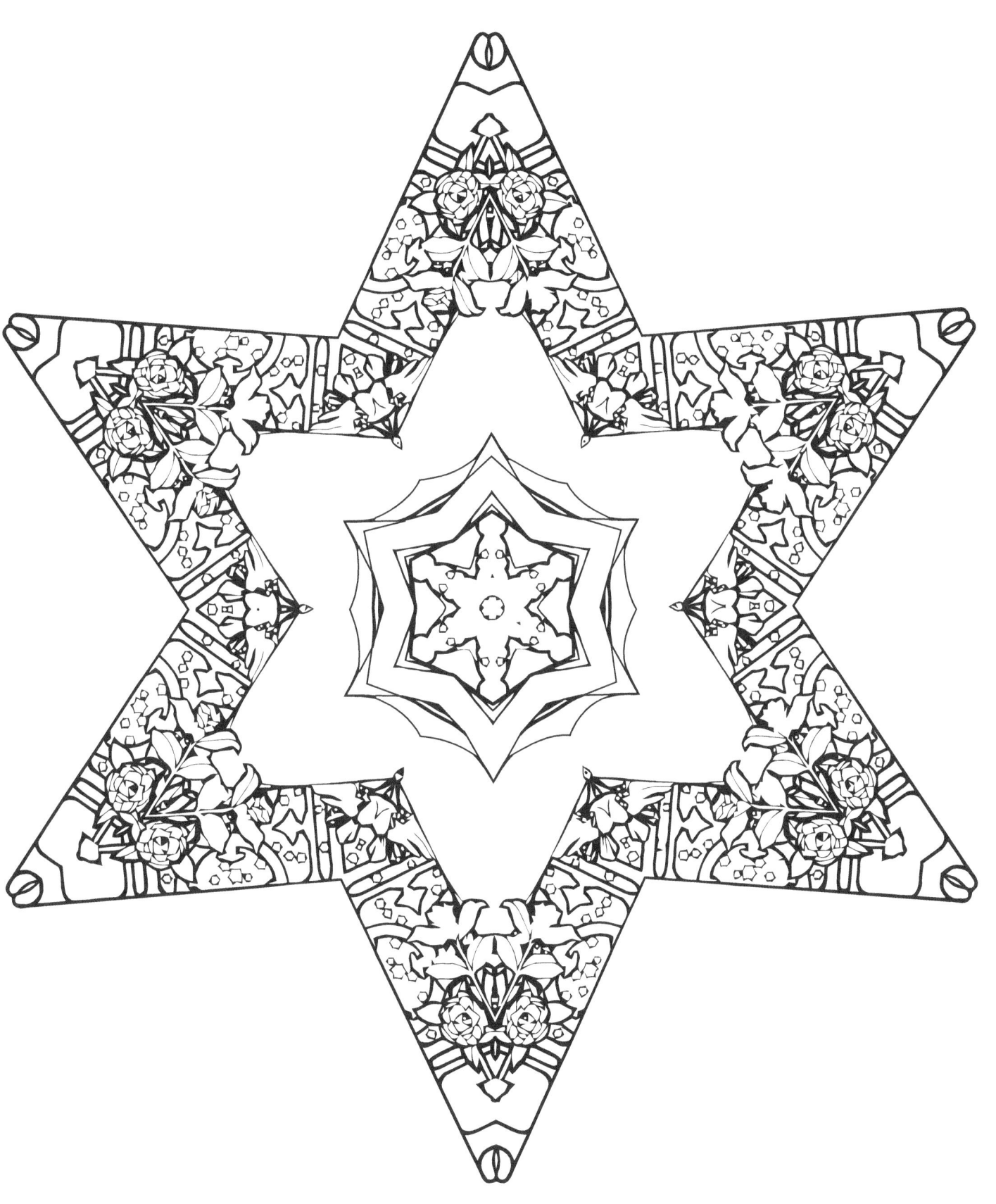

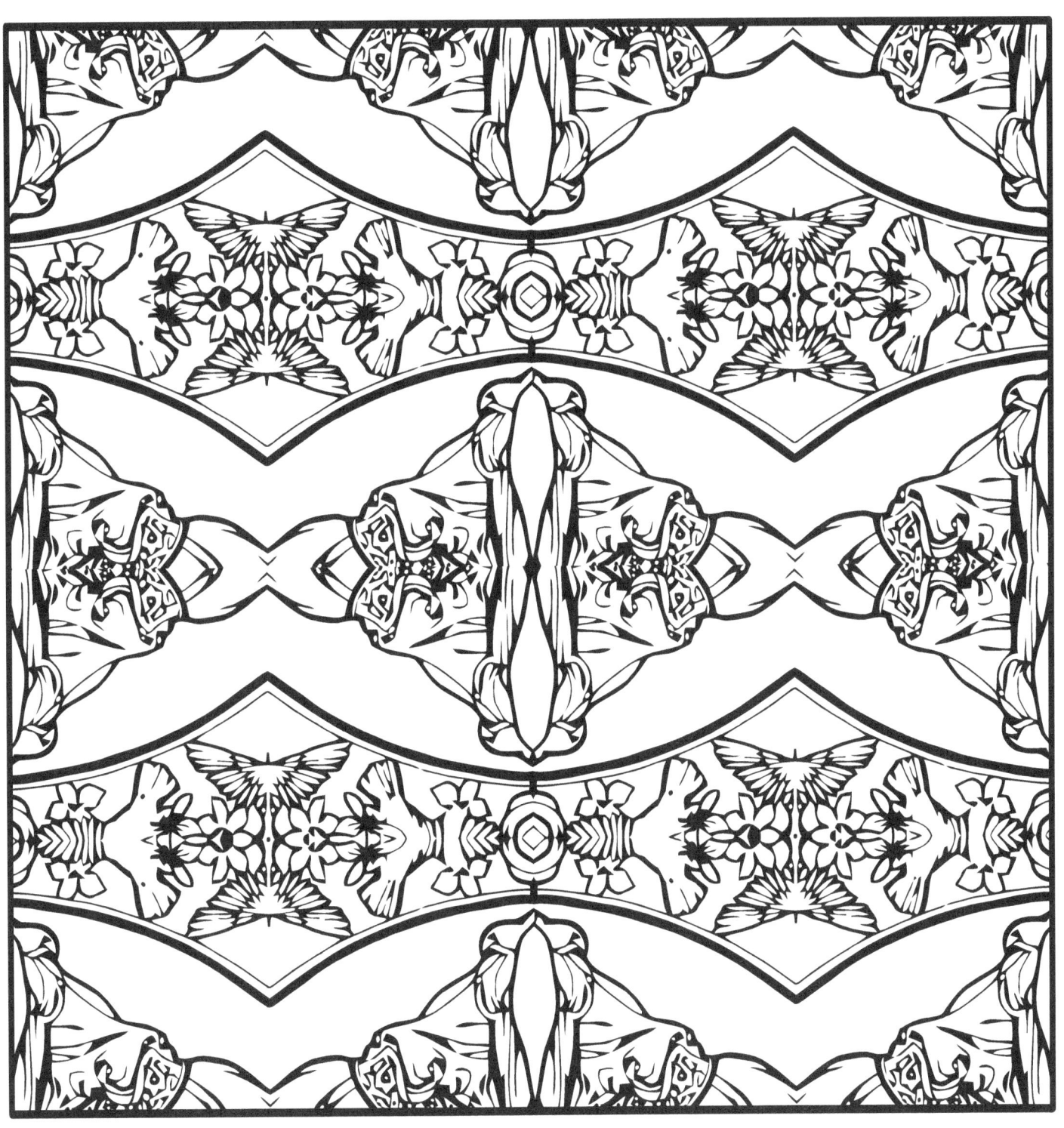

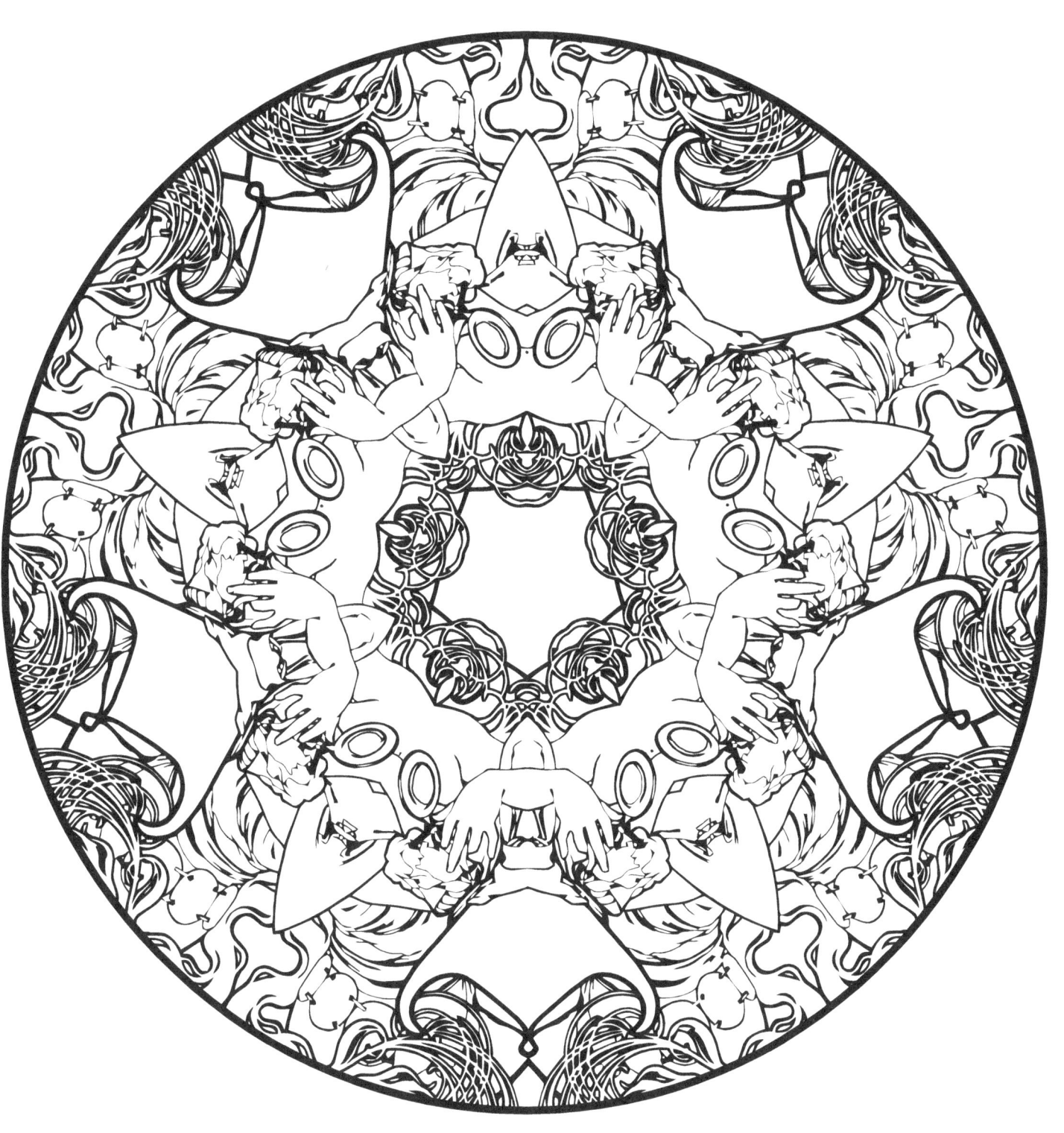

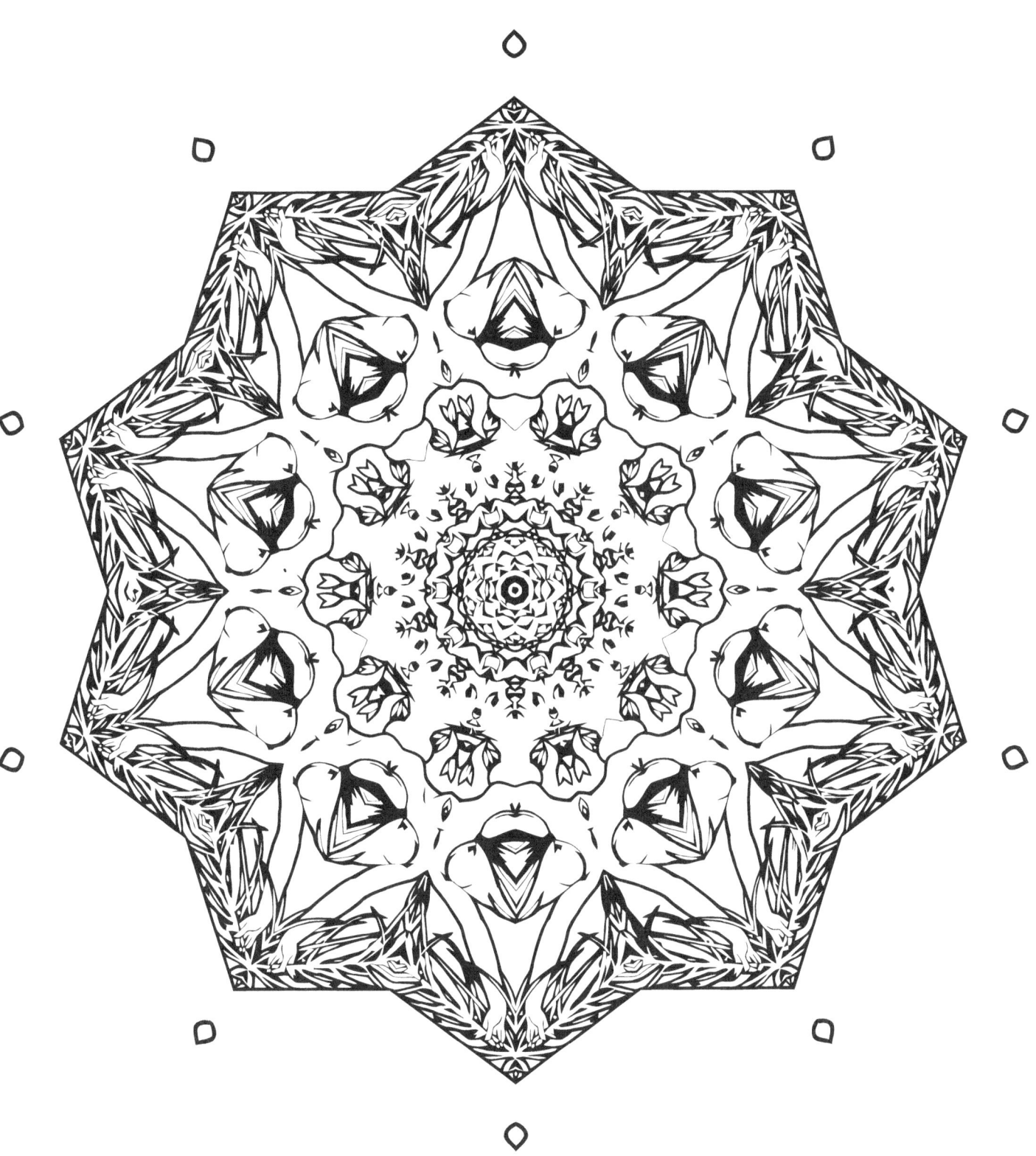

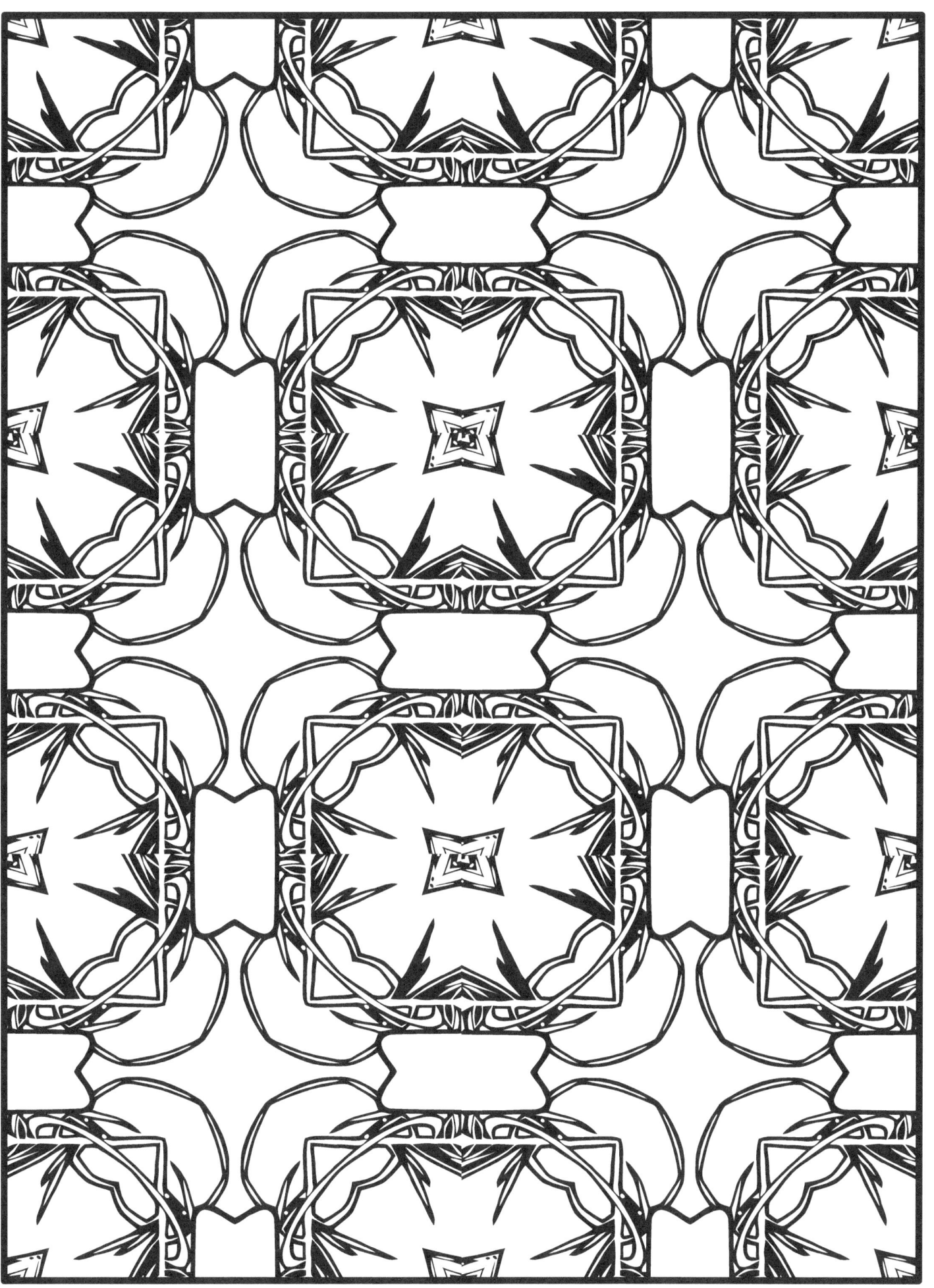

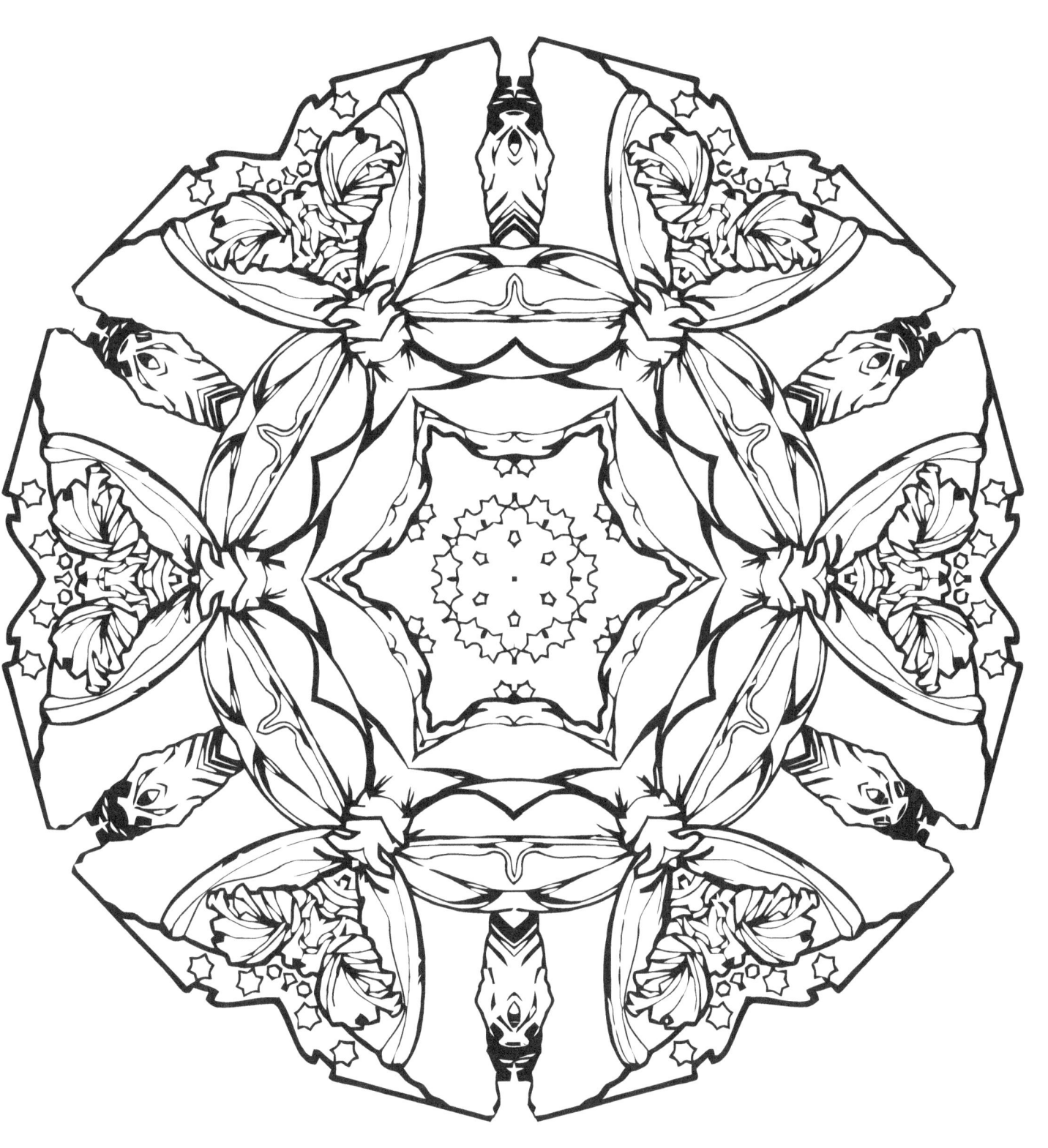

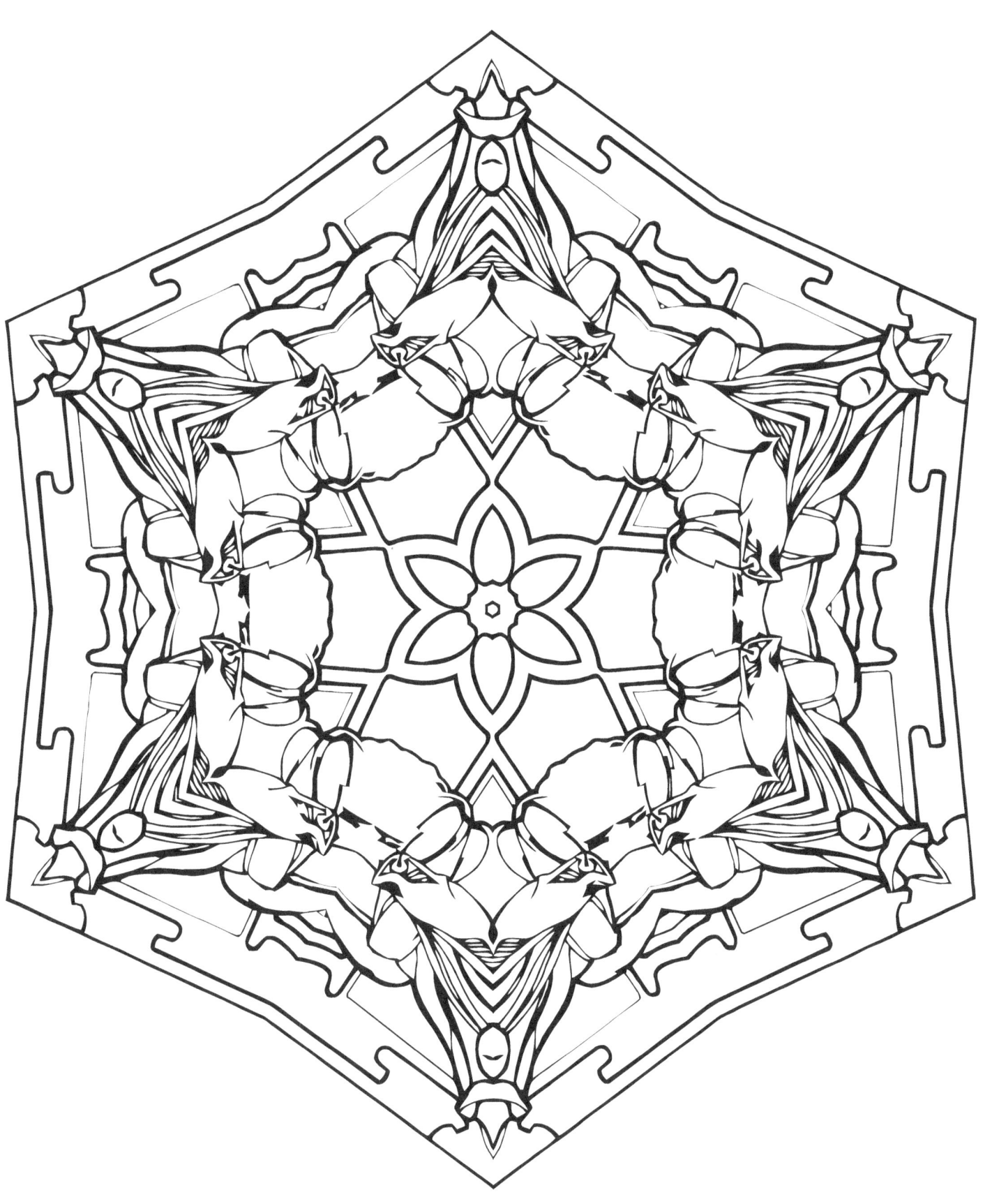

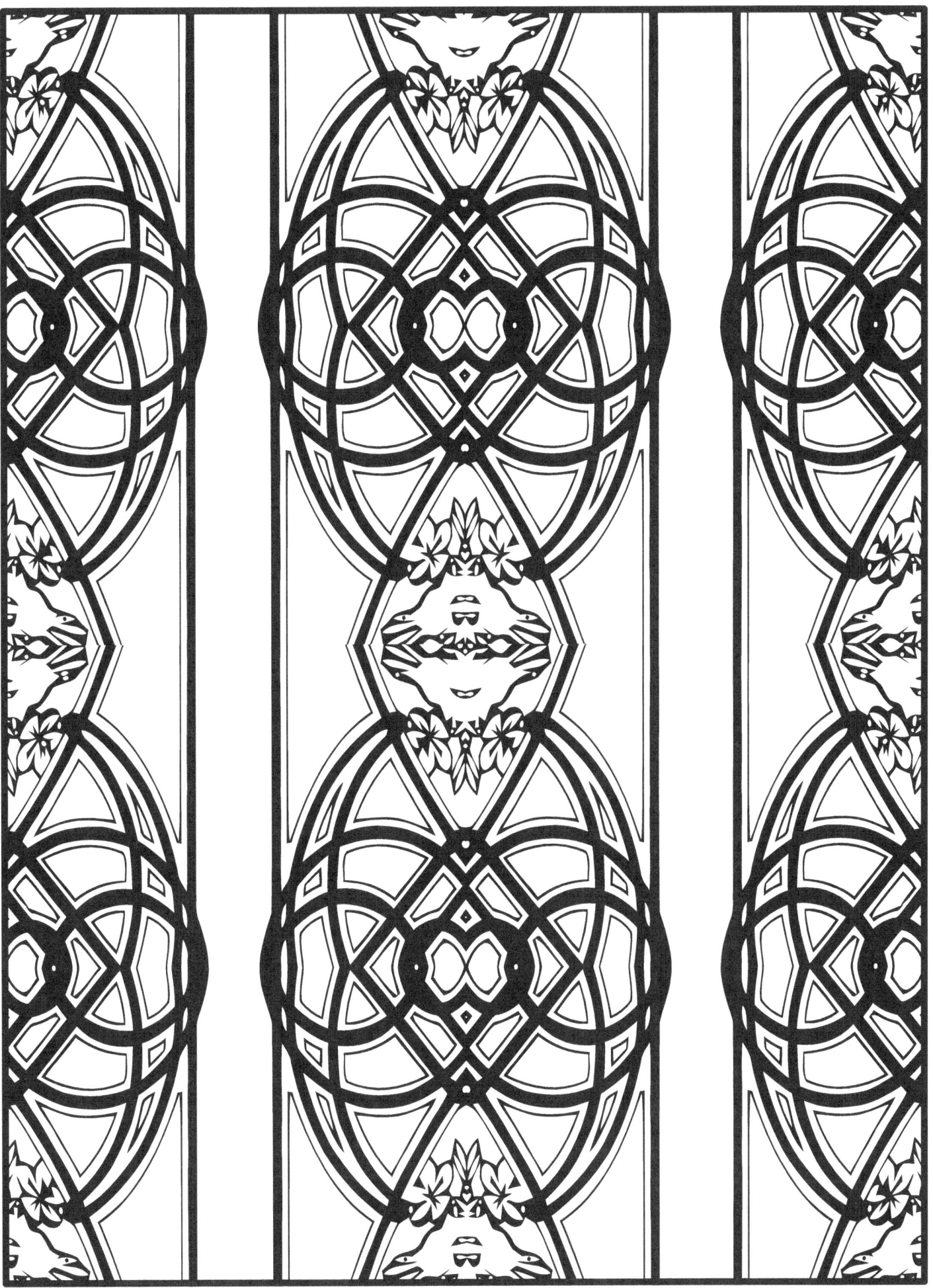

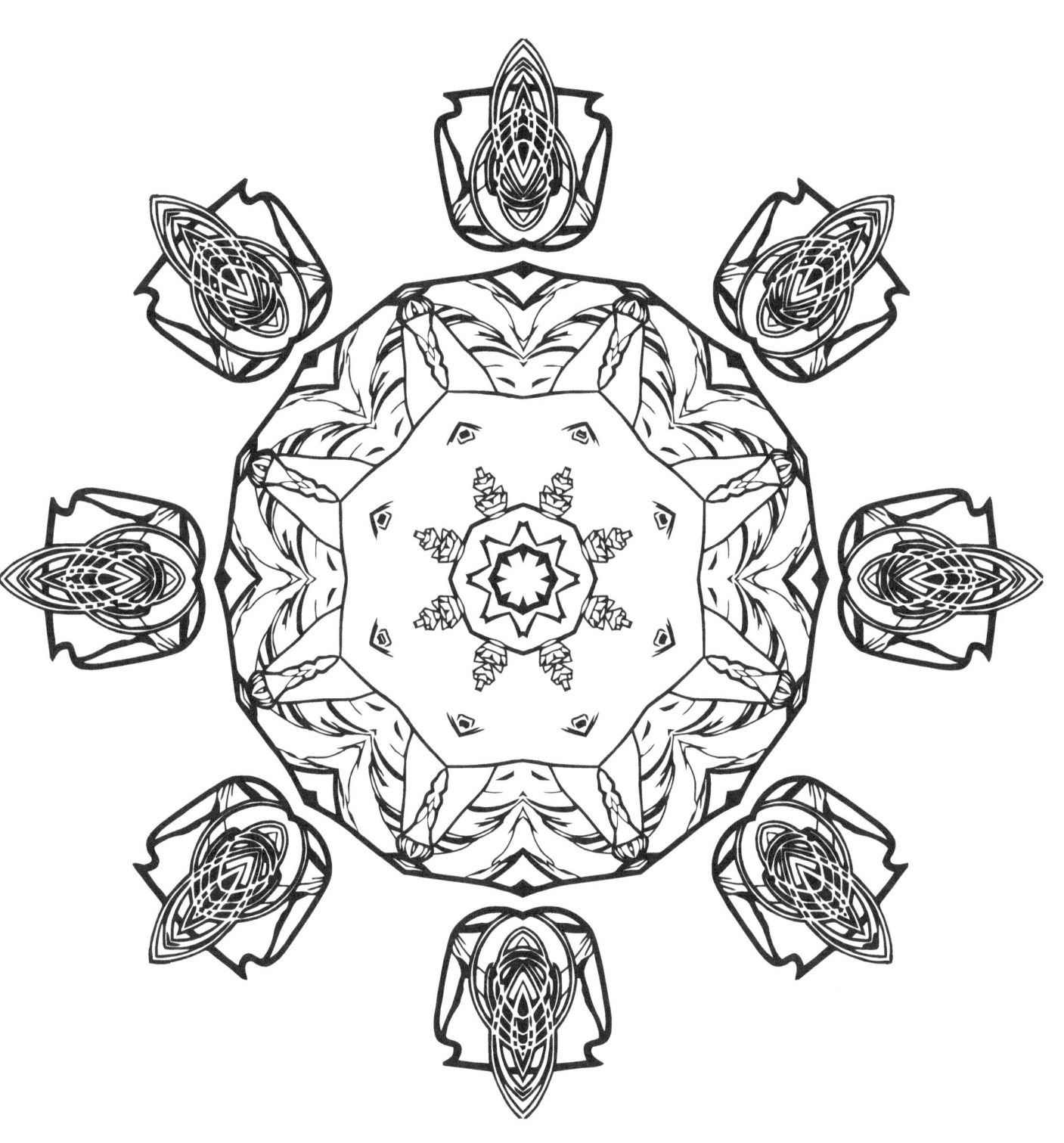

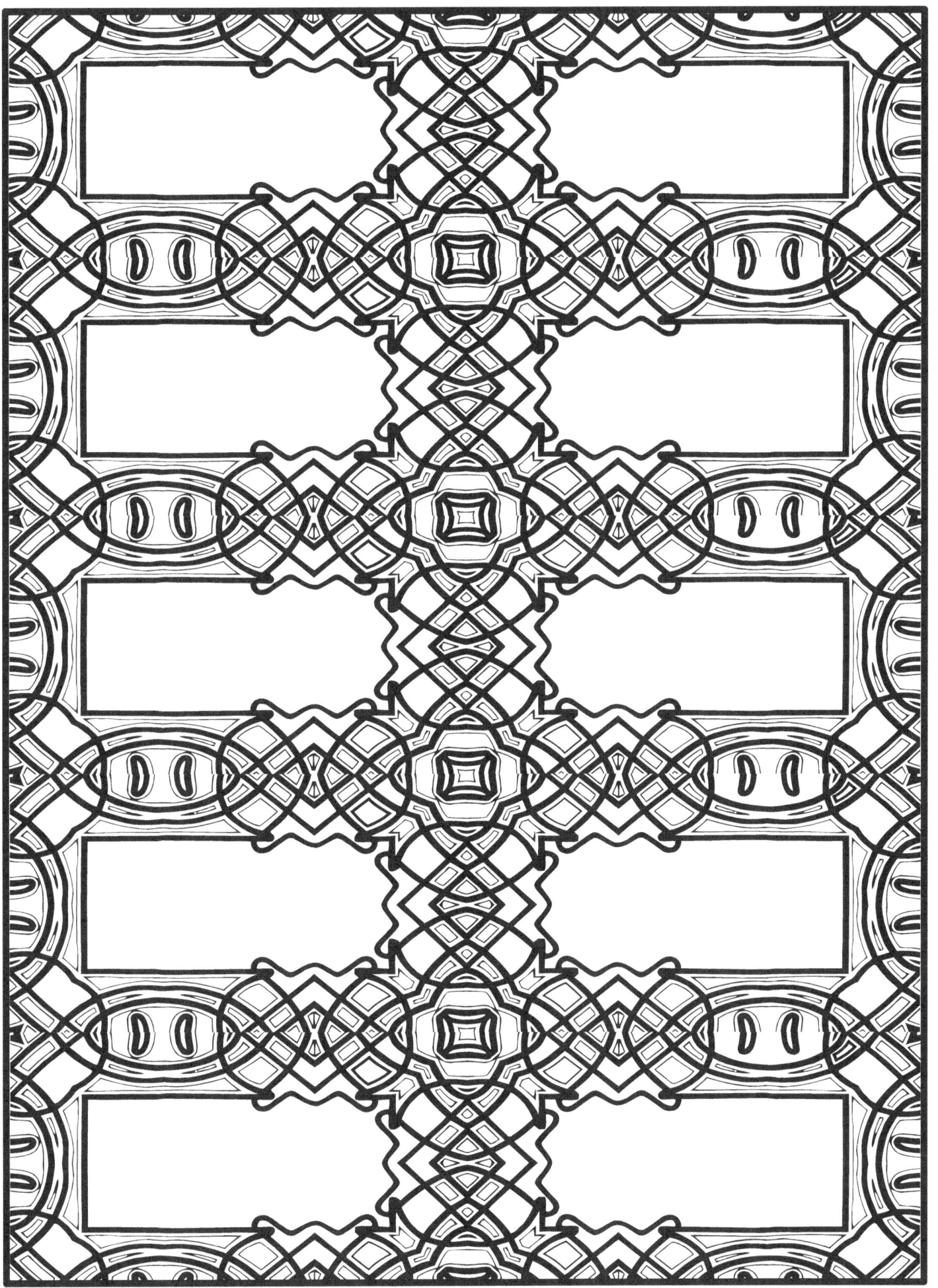

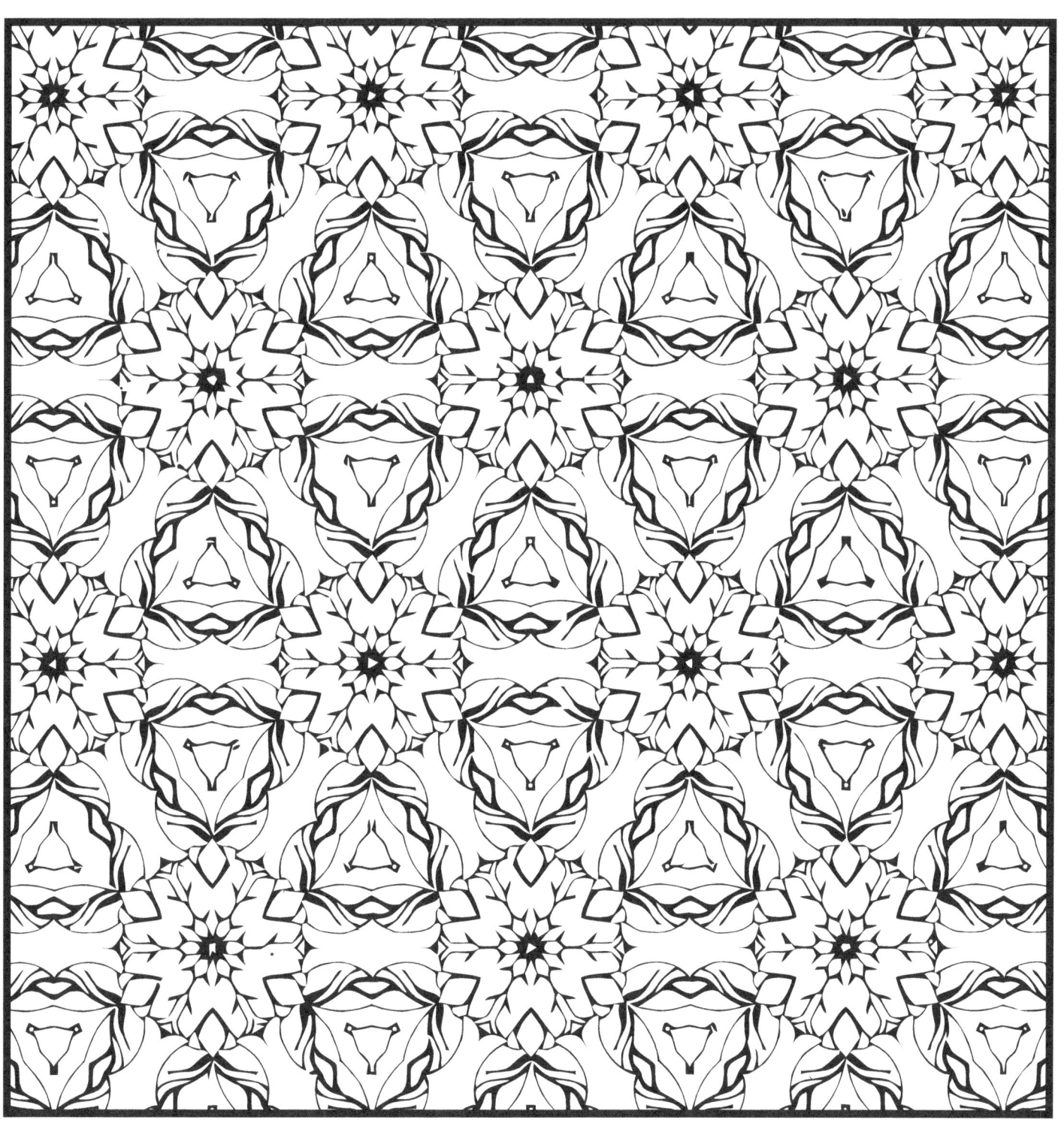

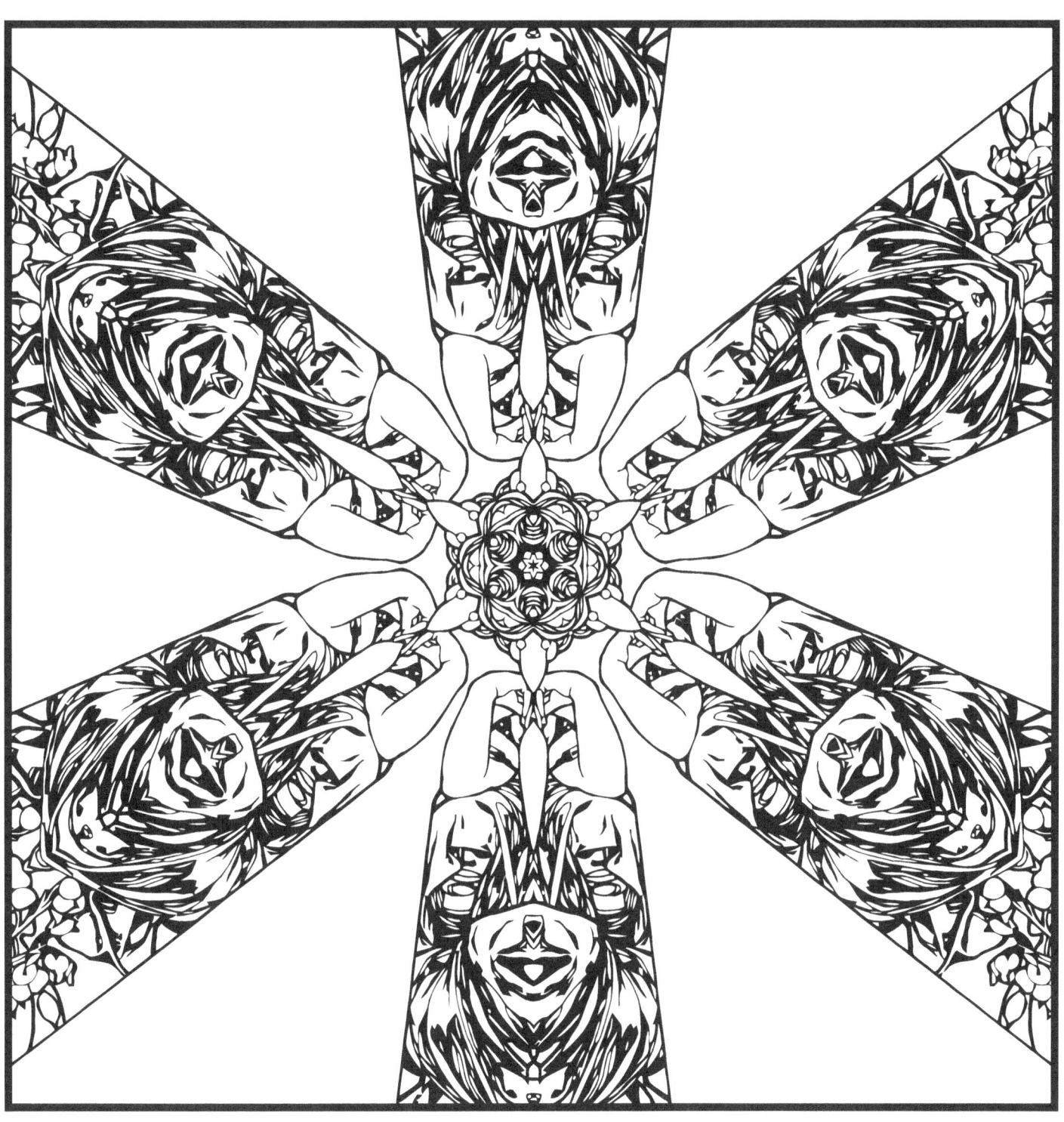

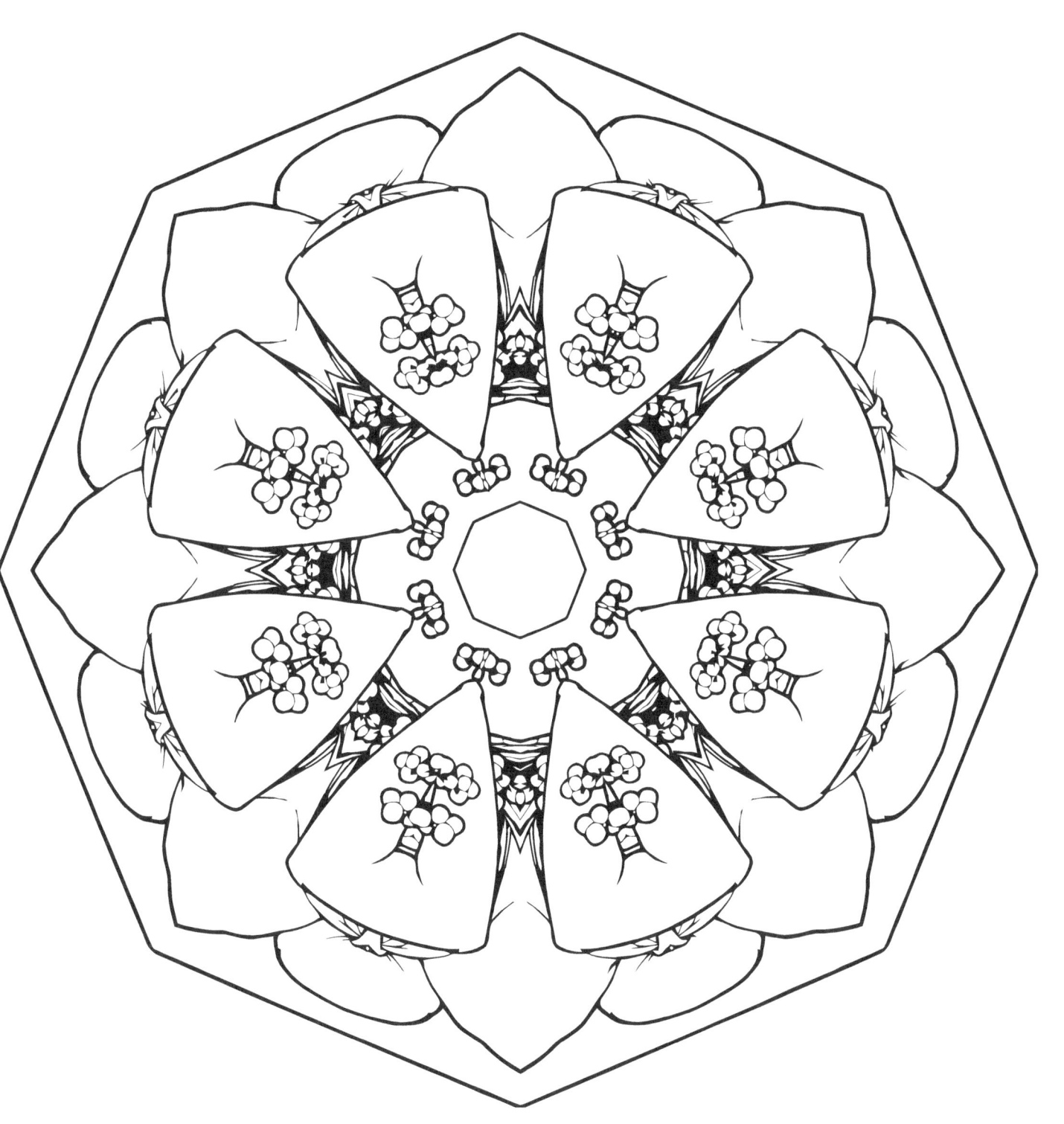

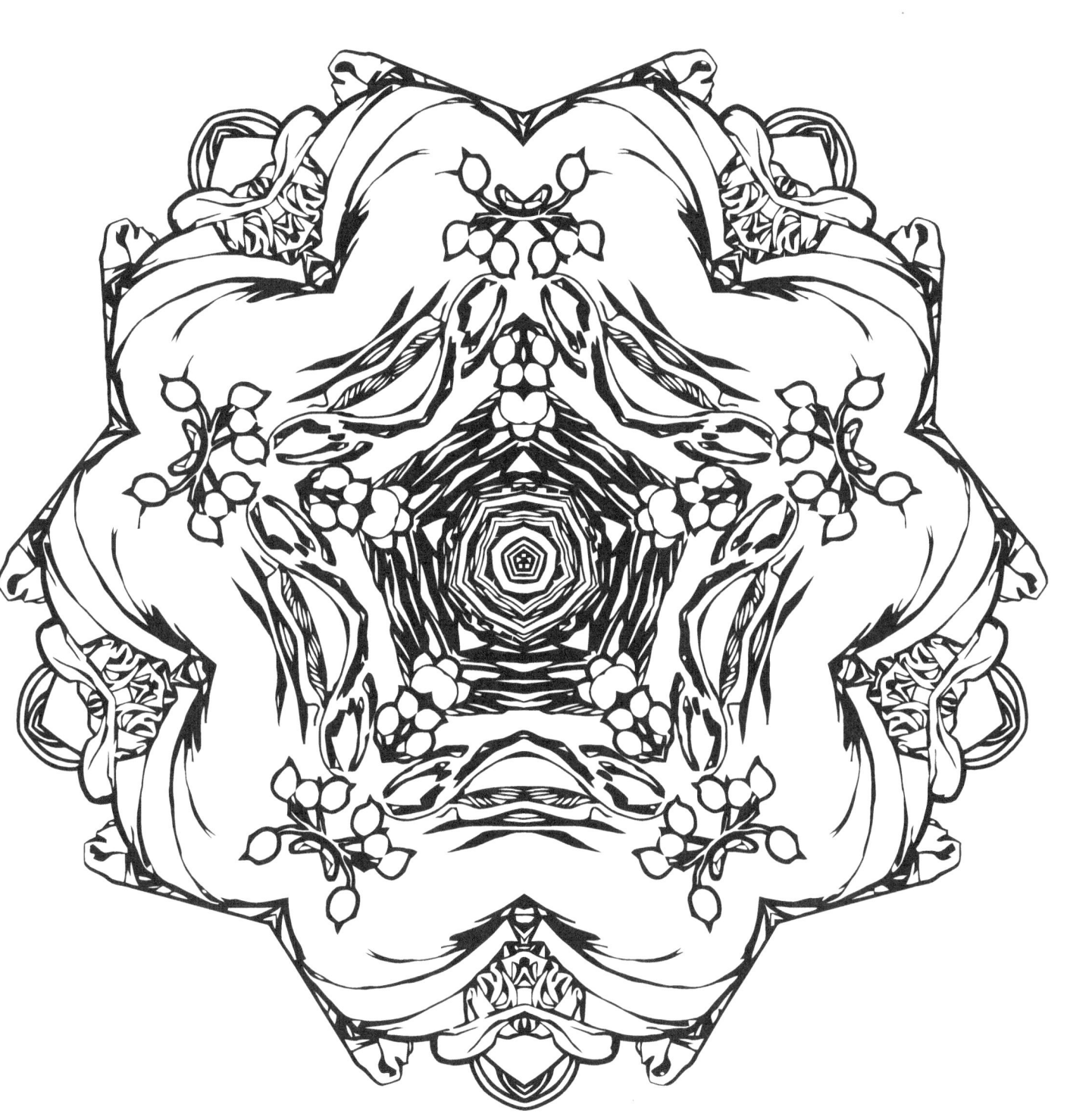

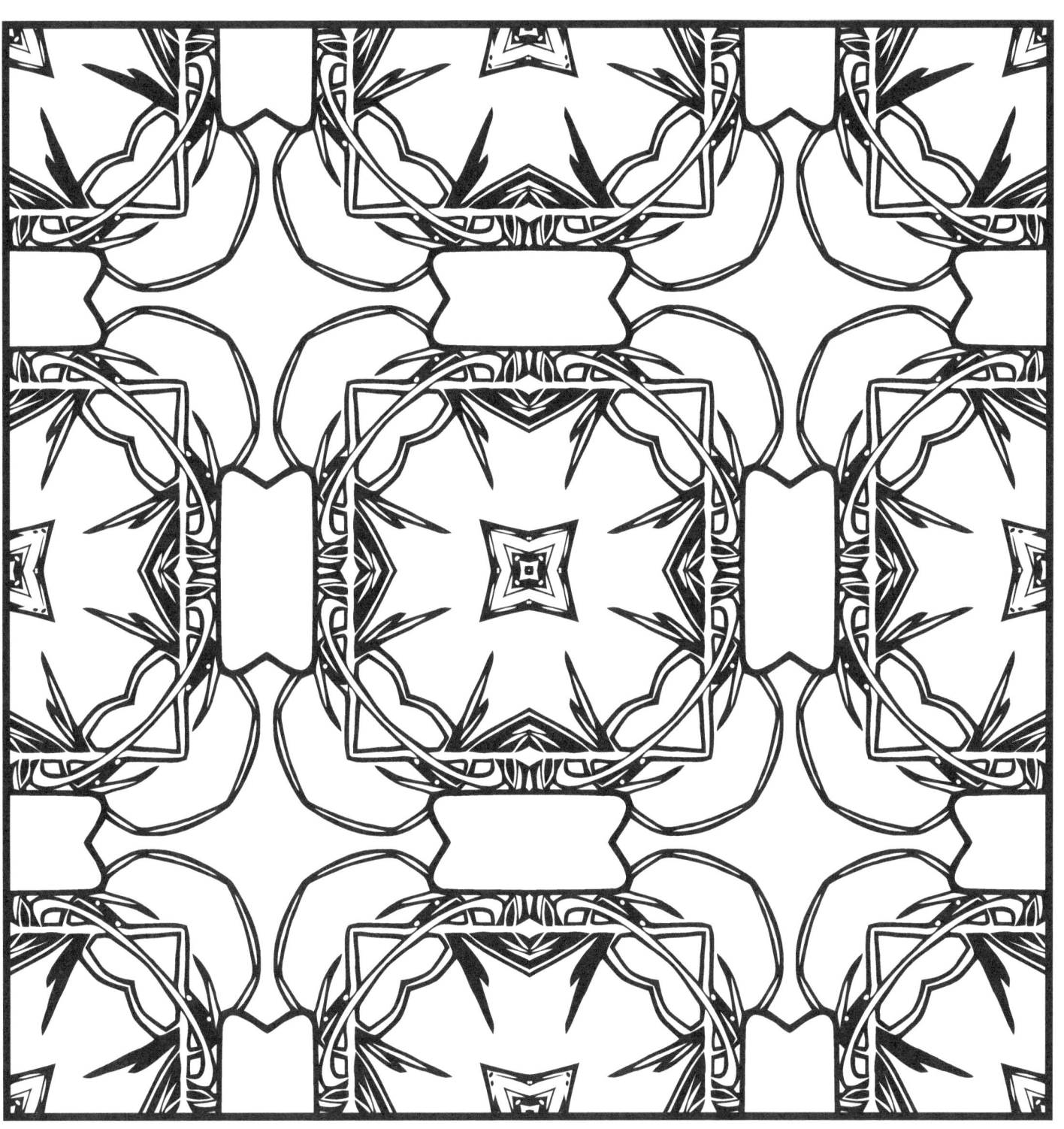

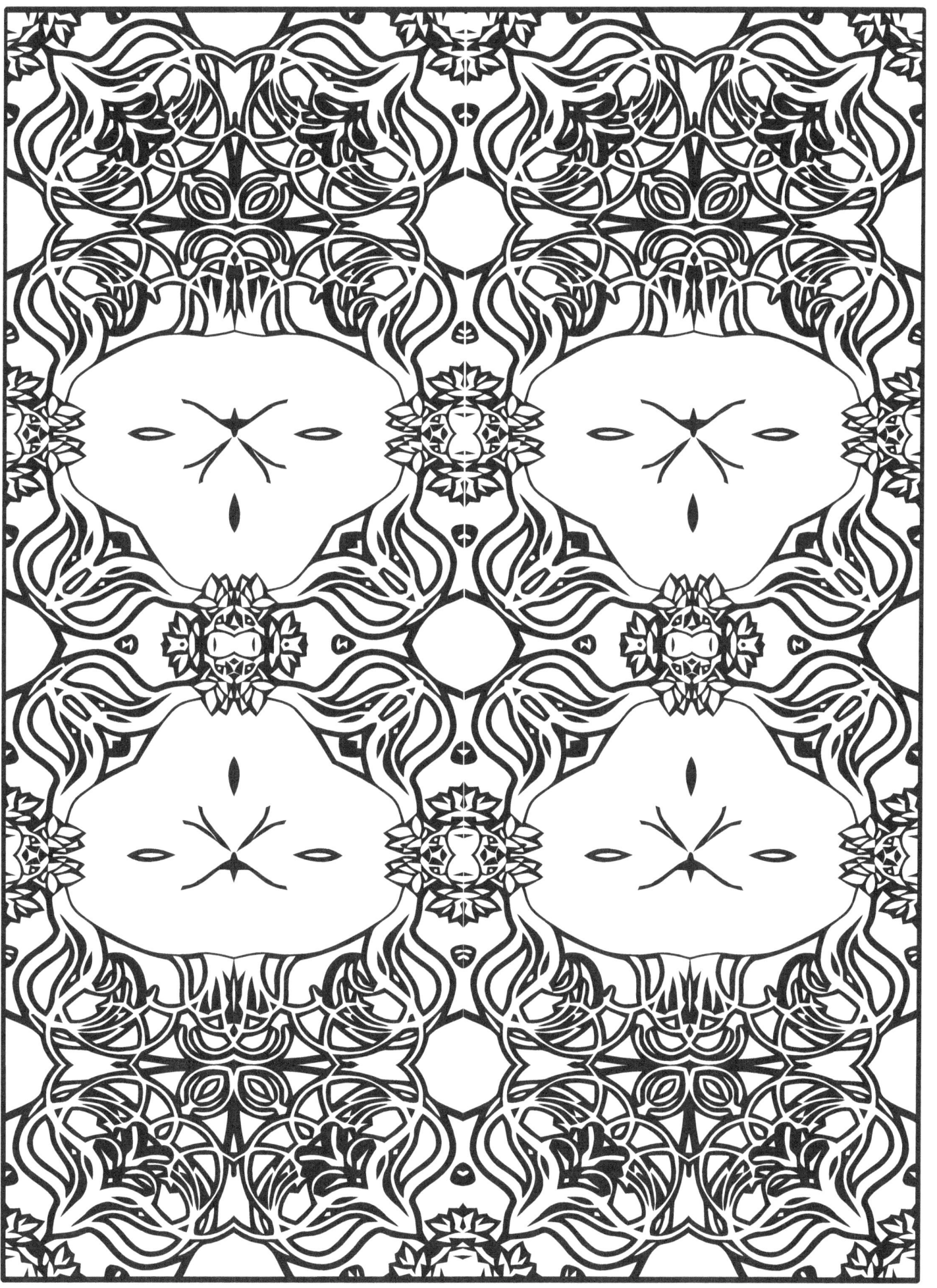

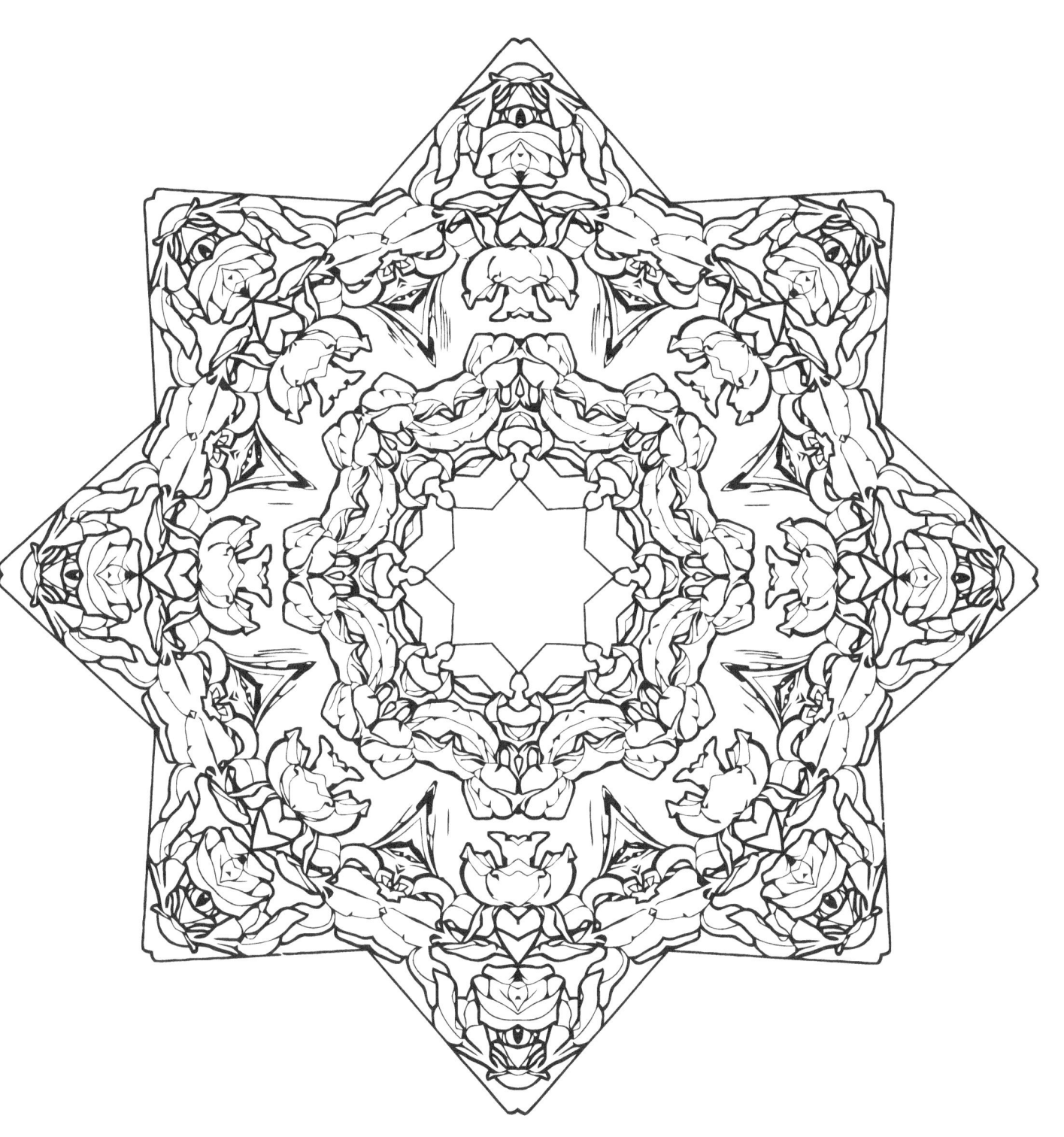

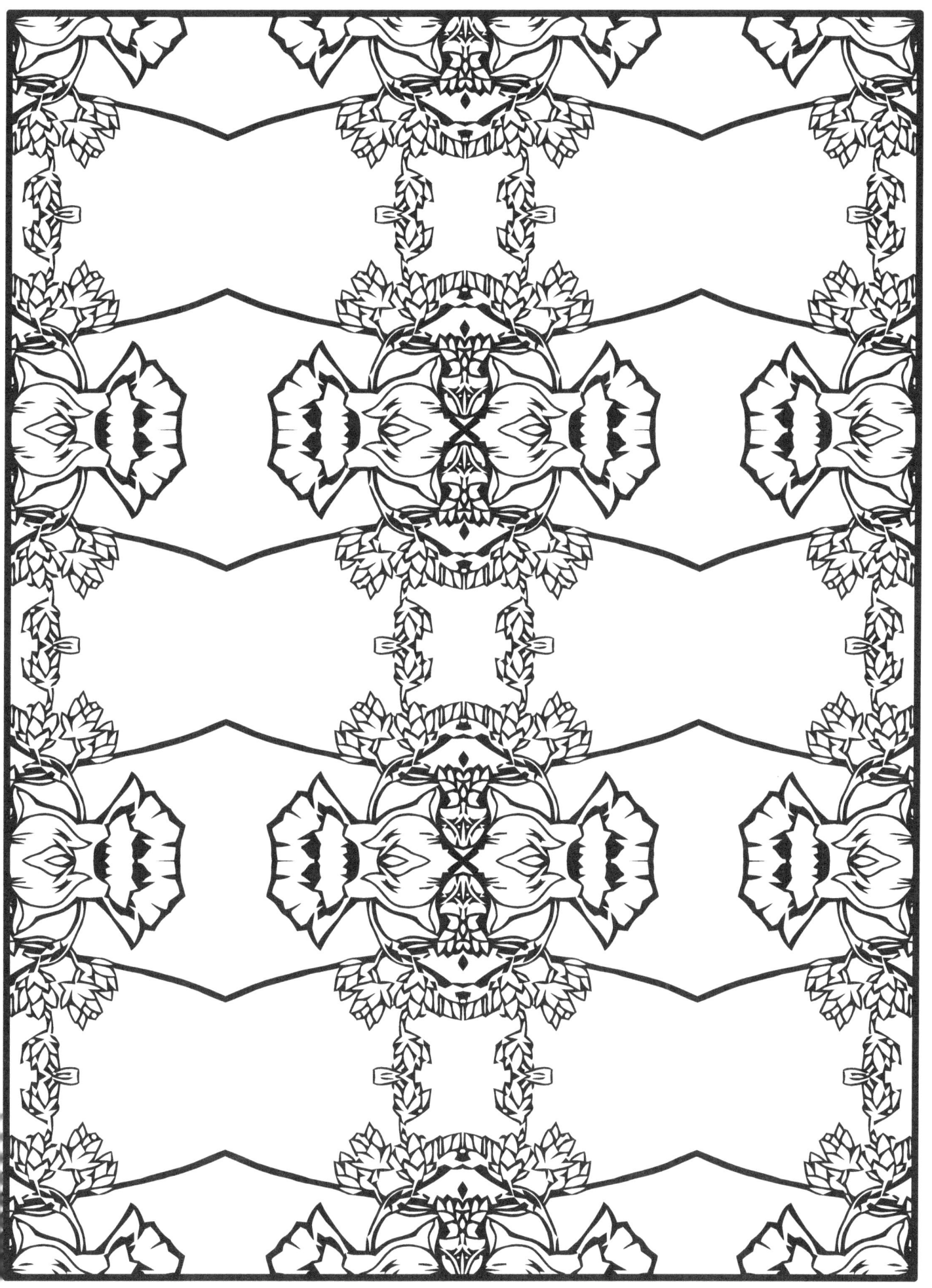

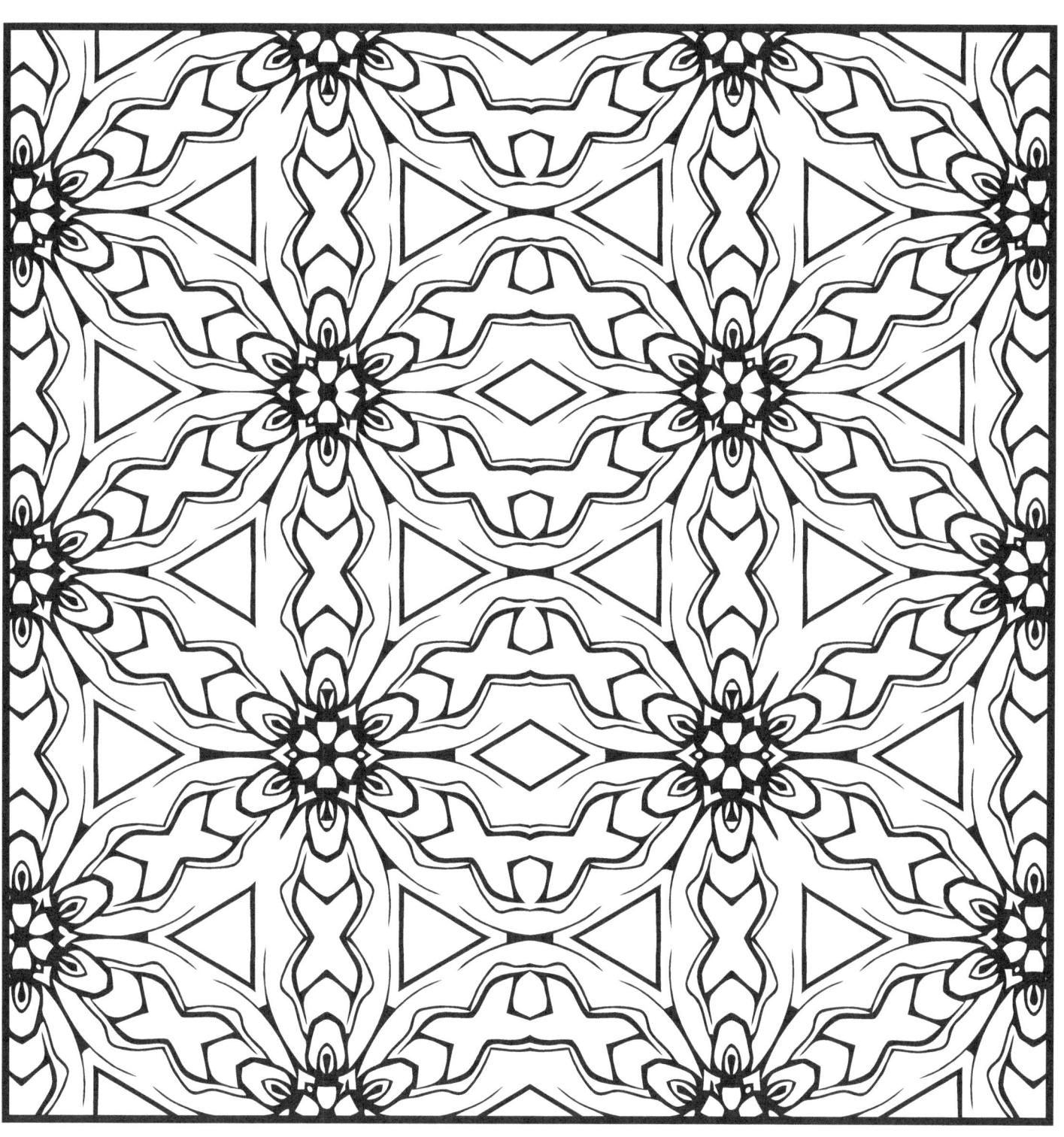

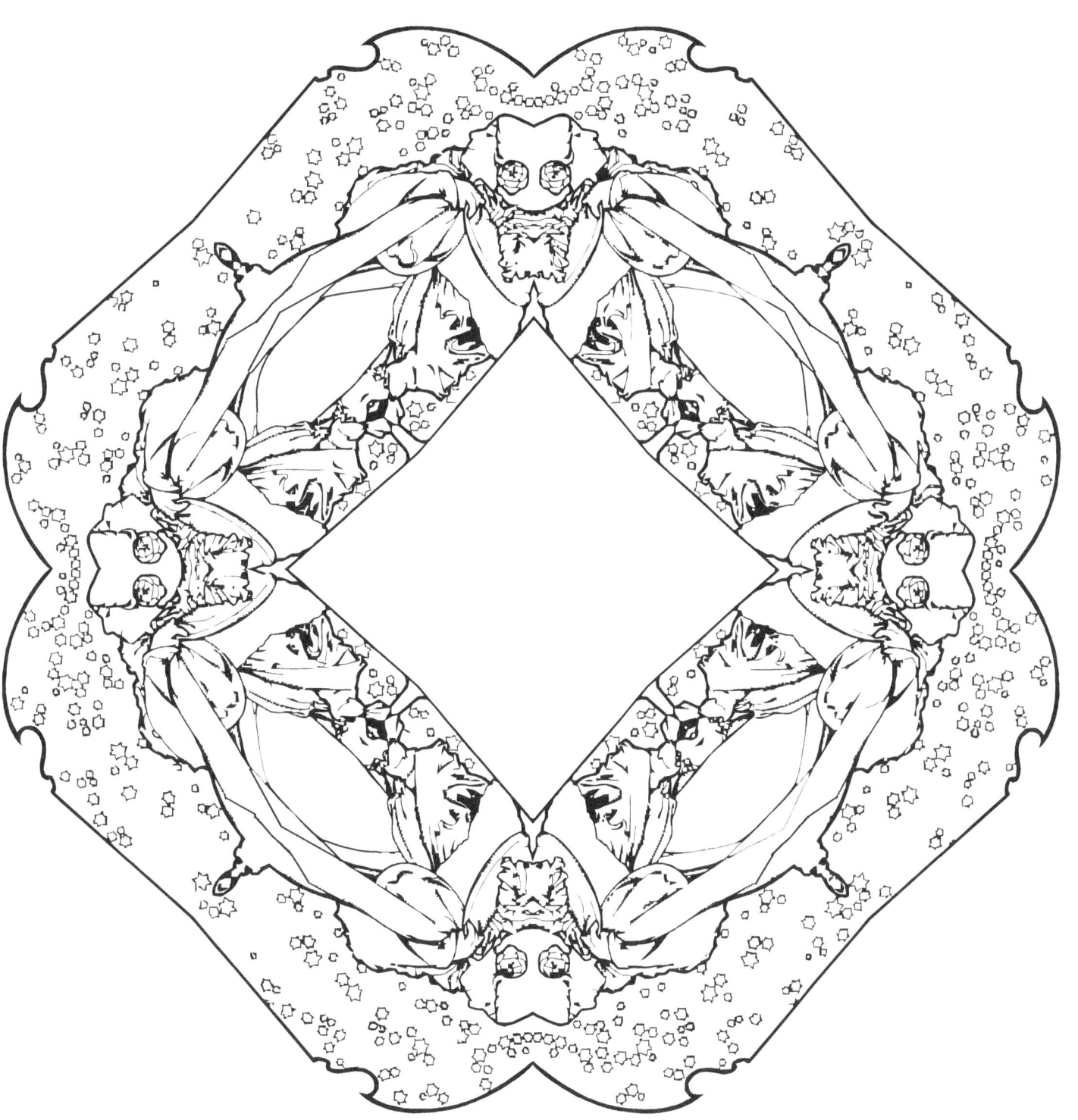

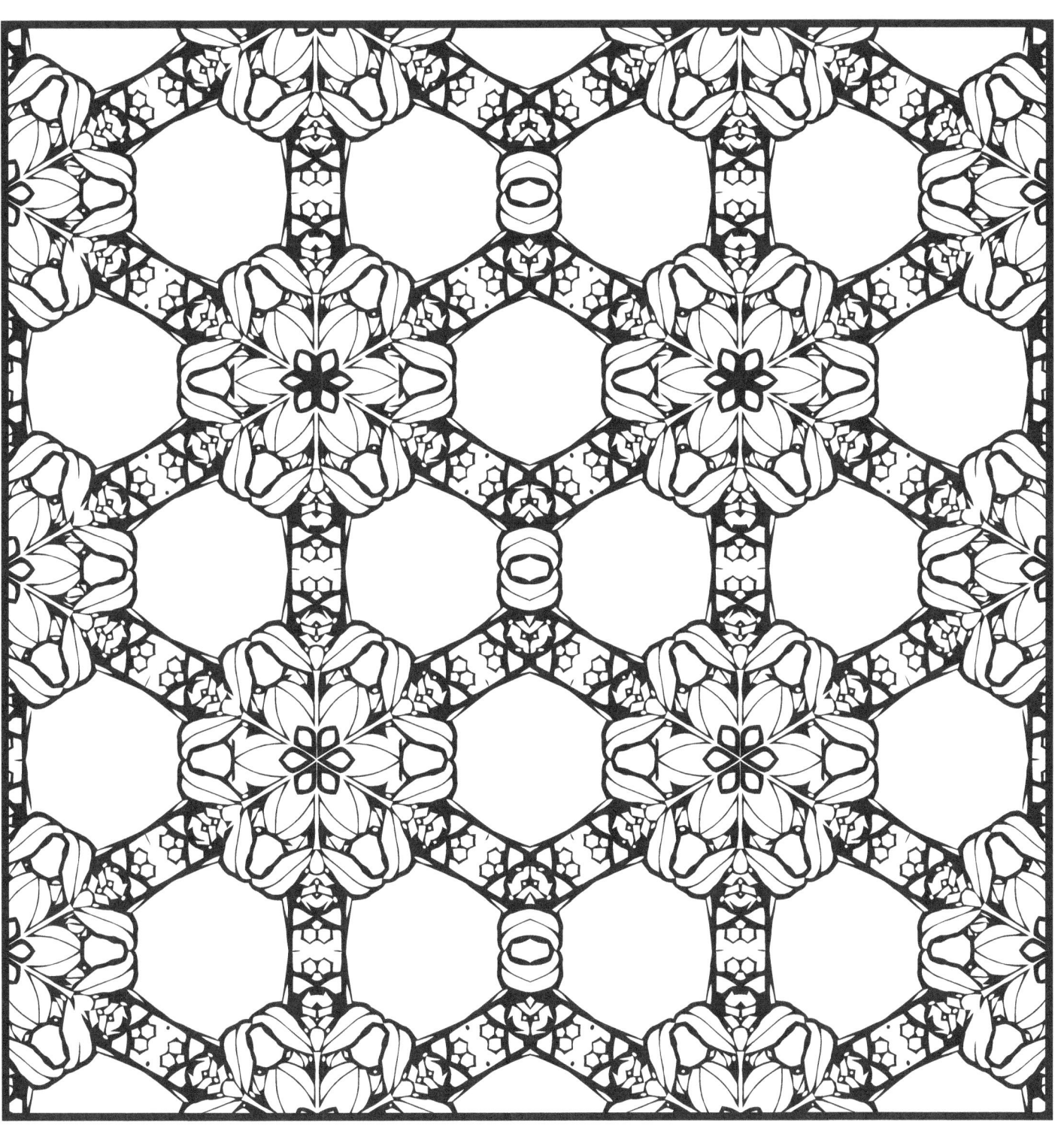

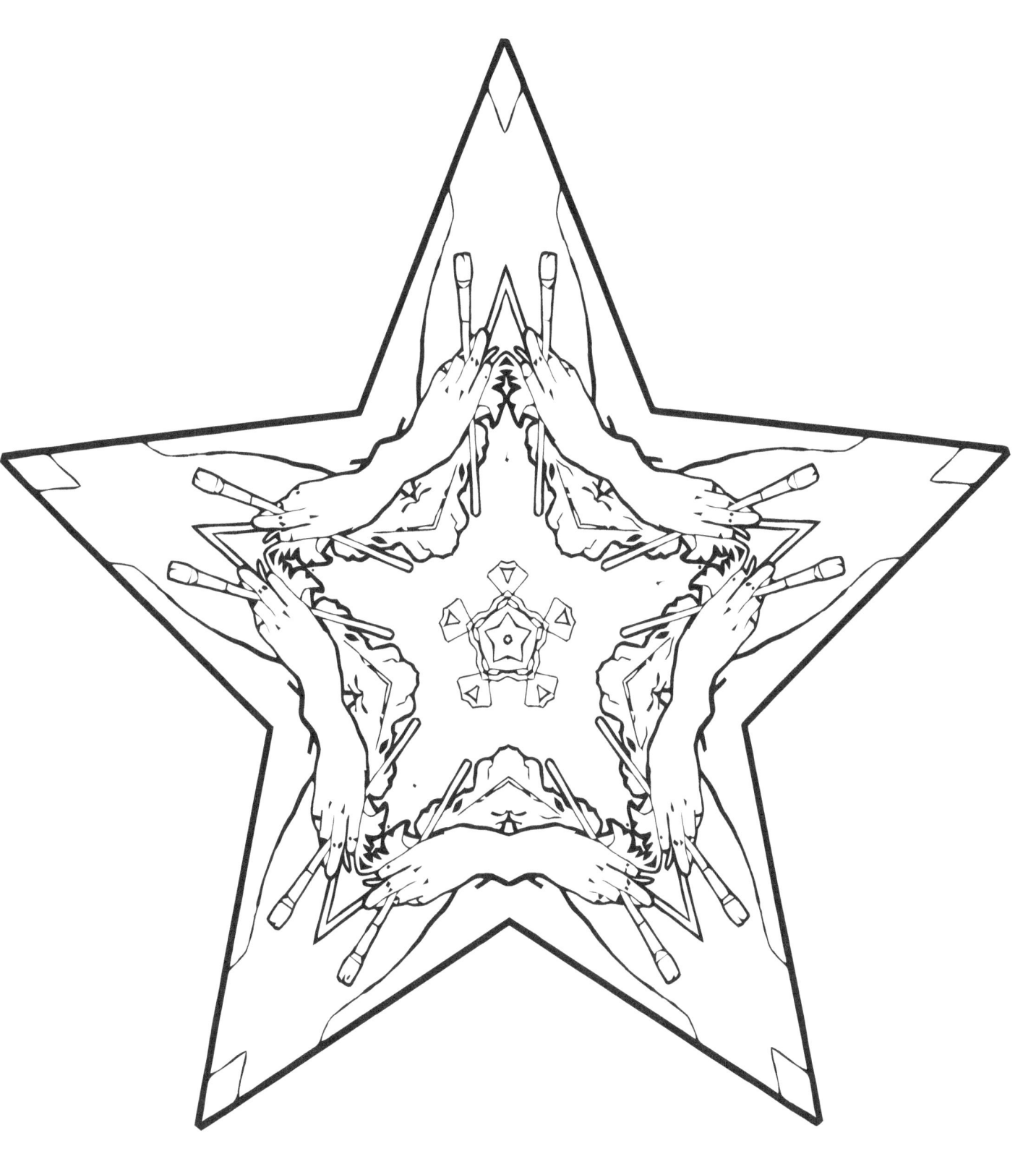

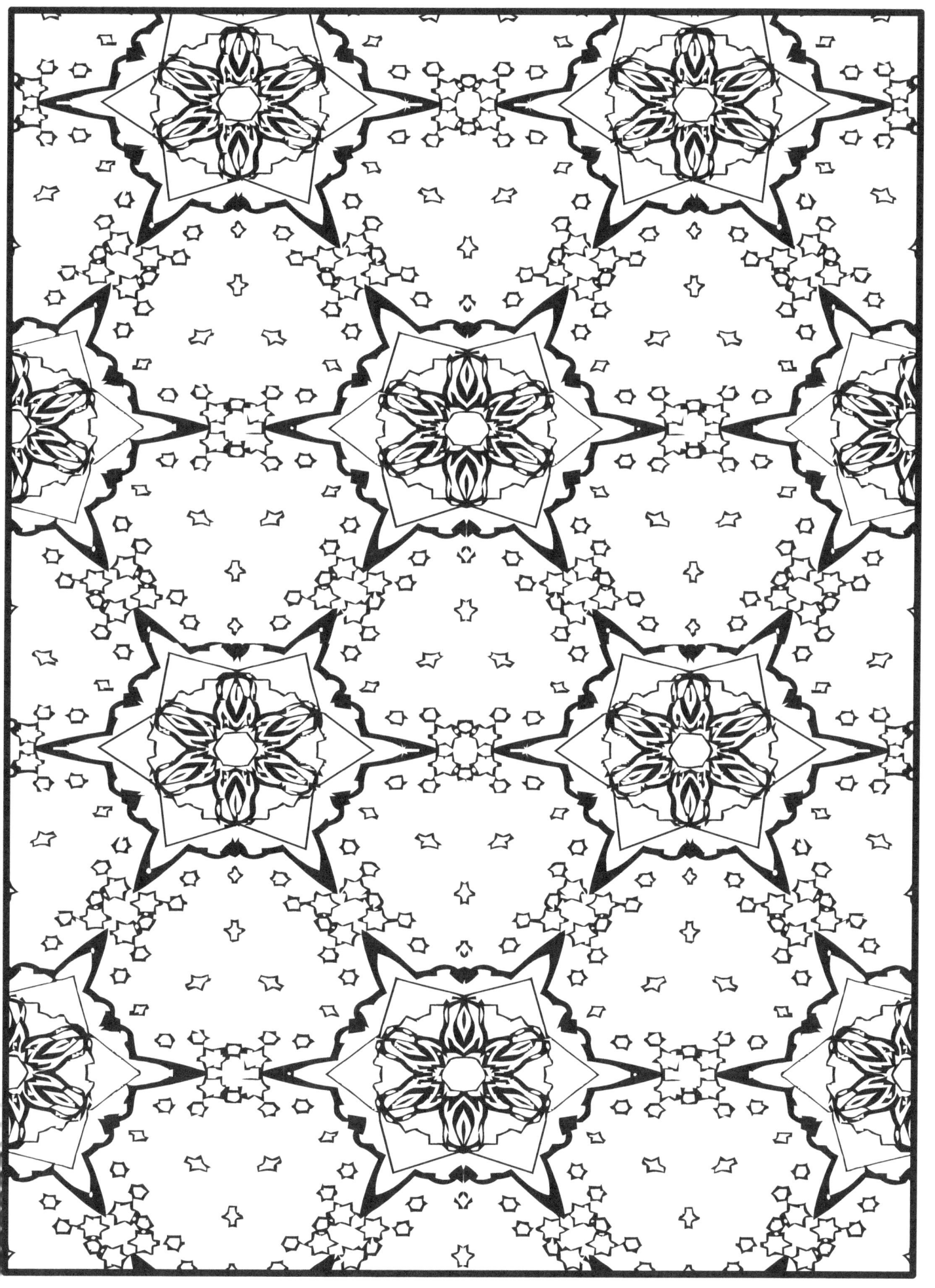

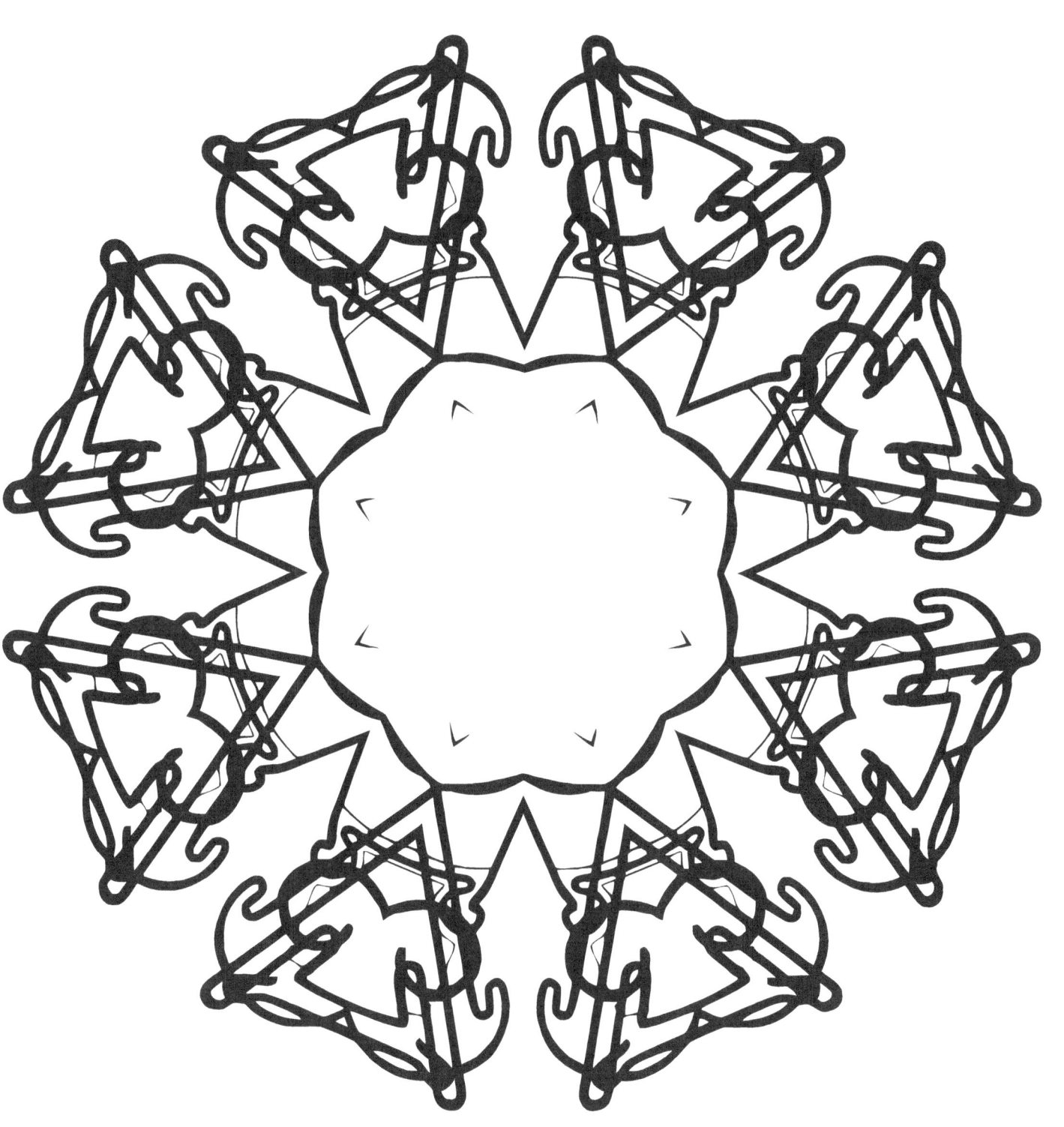

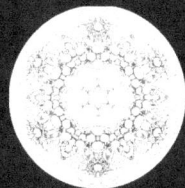
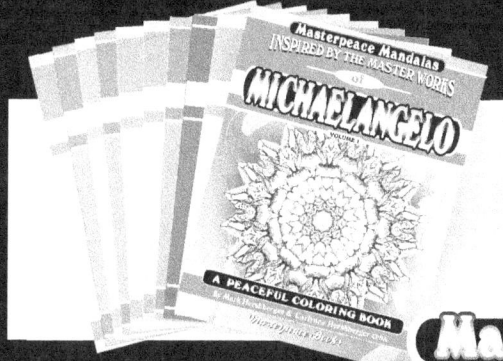

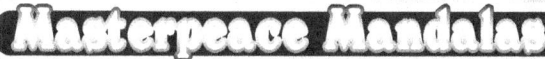
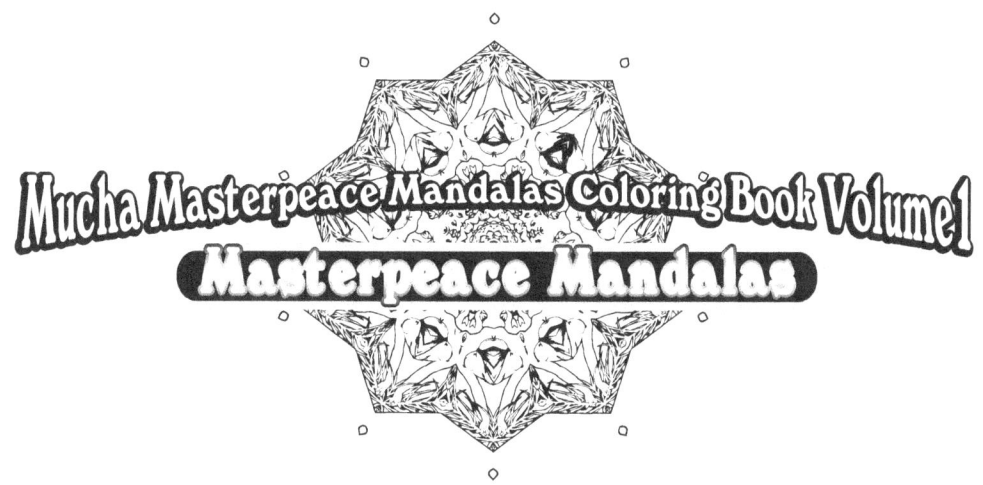